GROWING UP
IN A TOUGH CITY

GROWING UP
IN A TOUGH CITY

A Memoir

Jerry McGrellis

iUniverse, Inc.
New York Lincoln Shanghai

GROWING UP IN A TOUGH CITY

iUniverse books may be ordered through booksellers or by contacting:

iUniverse
2021 Pine Lake Road, Suite 100
Lincoln, NE 68512
www.iuniverse.com
1-800-Authors (1-800-288-4677)

The views expressed in this work are solely those of the author and do not necessarily reflect the views of the publisher, and the publisher hereby disclaims any responsibility for them.

The names have been changed to protect the guilty. Names have been changed to protect the real identity of the people on whom my characters are based. Times have changed—if you get into a fight today, you will probably wind up in jail. Do not try anything in this book because it could get you hurt or killed. This book is based on true events, but they did not happen in the exact time frame as written here.

ISBN: 978-0-595-42295-1 (pbk)
ISBN: 978-0-595-86632-8 (ebk)

Printed in the United States of America

This book is dedicated to Jesus, who died so my sins could be forgiven, to my mother Irene, whom I love with all of my heart, to my beautiful wife Karen, who has provided me with a lot of love, to my children Robbie, Monica, Kamila, Joey, Anthony, and Mia, who are my sunshine, and to Mickey Mellillo and all of my dear friends from Jersey City, whom I love and who are always in my heart.

Contents

Special Thanks

I give a special thanks to my friends,
Jed Dimatteo and Ade Makinde,
who have helped and encouraged me to write.

Chapter One:

Early Lessons

Jersey City, September 1966. It had just finished raining and a mist was coming up from the hot city street as the sun broke through the clouds. It was the end of summer and the first day of school but I told my mother I did not want to go. I was having too much fun watching TV and playing all day. My mother got my Catholic school uniform ready. The blue pants and white short-sleeved shirt did nothing for my chubby figure. I could never keep my shirt tucked into my pants, and my blue tie was always crooked. It looked like it was going to be a nice day, but for me, it was ruined. I did not want to go to school; my mother said it was time.

She got me dressed and combed my hair, the grabbed my hand, saying, "We have to leave for school now or you will be late."

Everyone walked to school. There were no school buses and most families had only one car that the father used to go to work. Some parents, like my mother, walked the children to school that first day, but after that, we were on our own. We had crossing guards and a police officer directed traffic on the corner, so we had a safe walk to school.

As soon as Mom and I left the house I started fighting her with all my six-year-old strength. I thought I had a slim chance to stay home from school if I put up a fight; maybe, at my age, school was optional. Mom told me I would have fun in school and meet new friends, but I fought with her the whole way to school, pulling my hand away and telling her over and over that I did not want to go to school. We had just moved to the neighborhood and I was afraid, because I did not know any of the kids in school. That would change quickly.

She had to drag me three blocks to rush me to school on time. When we turned the corner and I could see the school, I jerked my hand away to put up my last protest. She stopped in the middle of the sidewalk and said, "You are punished after school. You should not be giving me a hard time."

As soon as she said that I knew I should have given up sooner. I thought, *Great, not only do I have to go to school but after school, I won't get to go out to play because of the punishment.*

The exterior of St. Richard's School was brown brick. The building looked as if it had been there forever and it would last forever. The schoolyard was small, more of a parking lot than a schoolyard. All of the children had to wait there before the teachers would let us in the school.

When we got to the schoolyard, my mother kissed me and said, "Be good in school."

In those days, you never saw the nuns out in regular clothing. In their black habits and white wimples, they waited outside in the schoolyard for us, and once all the children had arrived, they lined us up and we marched into the school.

We started every school day with a prayer and the Pledge of Allegiance. The school walls were made of marble and the floors were hard wood. The desks were old and attached to the floor. The school was clean and everything was in place but what stood out to me were the names carved on the desks. The children before us left their markings on the desk. I would read all of the names, some of which were single names like Johnny and some of which were couples like Jacky and Mary. My mind wandered and I thought about how those kids had been able to carve their names in the desks without the teachers catching them in the act. I asked myself if they used scissors, knifes, or switchblades. I wondered if the kids in my class would carve their names in the desks.

I was six years old, but I will never forget that day as long as I live. That day started friendships that would last a lifetime. Most of the kids there knew each other from kindergarten. I just moved to the neighborhood and was new in school, but all the kids made me feel welcome. They were talking to each other and asking each other how the summer went and what they did on their summer vacations, when a freckle-faced kid said to me, "You're a new kid, what's your name?"

"My name is Tony," I said. "Nice to meet you."

"They call me Chubs. Pleased to meet you, too." Chubs was a nice kid, six years old like me, but he acted a lot older. He was the leader of the group. Chunky but not fat, with dark brown hair, he was one of the bigger kids in the class. I soon learned that he was the toughest kid in the class, but he really made me feel welcome. I found that out fast because as soon as the other kids realized I was new, they tried to figure out where I belonged.

One of the kids asked Chubs, "Where do you think the new kid would fit in on the list?"

"Don't worry about the list now; it's the first day of school and he's new," Chubs said.

I asked, "Chubs, what list?"

He said, "We have a list of the toughest kids in the class. We made it up in kindergarten." They had a rating system kind of like a ranking system in boxing, but there was no politics.

If you thought you were tougher than a kid who was higher on the list then you were, you challenged him to a fight after school. If the kid did not want to fight you, you took his place on the list and he went down to the next number. If you challenged a kid on the list for his ranking and he did not give it up freely you fought after school. It was important to be tough in Jersey City. Kids did not do a lot of bragging about how tough they were. If you thought you were tough then you had to prove it.

The list of the toughest kids was more important then the list of smartest kids. The smart kids usually were not cool, but Chubs was both tough and smart.

Some people just acted tough and some people really were tough. I guess that acting tough was a defense mechanism, like animals use in the wild. The small animals make themselves look big so the bigger animals will not eat them. Looking back, it seems crazy that you had to know how to fight in the first grade, but that's the way it was. It was like being in jail. You had to be tough or people would mess with you. We did not make the rules in Jersey City. We were only born there and we were trying to survive.

There was not much fighting for positioning for the toughest list. I made it to second place fast. Most kids talked tough but as soon as I told them I would meet them outside after school, they would give me their place. In third grade, I did have one fight after school when a new kid thought he was tougher than me. He was a nice kid, but we had to fight. We met after school, and it was just him and me—no crowd. I punched him in the face and he grabbed my leg and took me down. The priest saw us fighting and came over to break it up. We told him we were just practicing fighting. We called the fight a draw and we shared the second toughest place. I never challenged Chubs; I liked him too much and I was not sure about my chances of beating him.

That first day, we hadn't been in class very long before the teacher had to leave the room for a minute. "I will be right back," she said as she left the room. As soon as she left, Patty, a little skinny blond-headed kid, stood on his chair and started singing, "Three little black boys sitting in a bed, one rolled over and the other one said, 'I see your hiney, it's nice and shiny, you better hide it before I bite it.'" The whole class was on the floor laughing. Patty was a tiny little kid, a tough kid, but his specialty was comedy. Patty loved making us laugh. As soon as he was done with that song he started singing about the monkey that wrapped his tail around the flagpole to see his asshole. Patty saw the teacher coming back to the class and sat down. We were all smiling but the teacher did not know what had been going on while she was gone. Patty kept a straight face as he made believe he was reading a book. I did not know where Patty learned the songs but we all learned things from each other, and we all learned fast.

You had to learn fast in Jersey City, because the city moved fast.

The bell ended the first day of school and I walked home. My mother asked me how I liked school. I told her about all of the friends I met. She said, "I knew you would have a good time and make friends."

I said, "Could I go out to play now, Mom?"

"No, you are being punished; you have to stay in the house today," she said. I learned not to give my mother problems getting ready for school. She explained that children have to go to school every day to prepare to go to work every day. The same people that find excuses not to go to school will find excuses not to go to work. "If you cannot get up to go to work, you will not be able to support your family and your children will not have food to eat," she said. Mom always took time to teach me important lessons, even if I didn't know then that they were important. This was only one of the important lessons I learned in Jersey City.

There were two separate worlds in Jersey City, one for adults and one for kids. The adults did not know what the kids did in their world and us kids kept things in our world to ourselves. In both worlds, however, there was nothing worse than a rat. You learned to keep your mouth shut, fast. You even learned that in the house; my mother would tell me to mind my own business and warn me not to tell on my friends. That unwritten code was enforced and you would get your butt kicked if you broke it. Even the nuns and priest looked down on tattle-tales. Children in my neighborhood were taught to be loyal to our friends and that meant keeping our mouths shut if a friend did something wrong. You could tell your friend he was wrong to his face, but you could not tell on him.

Both nuns and lay teachers taught at St. Richard's School. Our parents figured that we were better off in Catholic school because the public schools were tougher and you did not have a good chance of learning anything. I did not learn a lot of reading, writing, and arithmetic in school but the nuns and the priest did teach us a lot about life. I think they saved my life with those lessons. They taught us about God and Jesus, and that alone could get you through any situation, even growing up in Jersey City. They taught us the Ten Commandments, which we translated into our own version: "Love God first because he was the boss and he sent Jesus to die for us." Anybody that would die for you really loved you and had guts and we really respected that. The nuns taught us to love our neighbors, and to us that meant we had to love our friends and watch out for one another. The nuns tried to teach us that we had to love everyone, but that was a little too much for us to comprehend, so for the time being we got by with loving our friends—and that was only if they were doing the right thing. If your friends were not doing the right thing, they deserved to get their butts kicked. However, for the most part, the nuns taught us to take care of each other and because of that, we knew we could count on our friends when we needed them. The nuns taught us not to mess with somebody's wife, and for us that included girlfriends. We had our own little rules about the commandment that read, "Do not steal"—it was worse to steal from poor people than from rich people. Stealing from big stores or big companies was wrong, but not as bad as if you stole from poor people. I learned that not stealing was still a commandment from God and if you broke it, you would pay. "Thou shalt not kill" we read as, "Don't kill unless you don't have a choice or unless somebody threatens your family or friends." Go to church. Obey your mother and father unless they are real nuts and they tell you to do bad things. The nuns taught us that if we wanted God to love us, we had to love God. In a crazy city, they really gave us good guidelines for living.

Some of the nuns were tough. They were not afraid of anything, and they didn't duck the tough questions. If you asked them a question, they answered you. One kid asked them about the Ten Commandments. "Do you still have to obey your parents if they are nuts and tell you to do bad things?" The nuns would say no. To us, they were authority from heaven so we listened to them. My biggest question was who made God. I could not get the concept, but they told me it was a mystery and we just had to have faith in God. They told us we would feel him in our lives if we did the right thing.

Our parents considered nuns as holy. In Catholic School, the nuns had a license to kick your butt, and if you needed it, they'd kick it. If you got your butt kicked in school by a nun, your mother and father would kick it again if they found out about it. You were better off just taking the nun butt-kicking to save yourself the butt-kicking by your parents. It was a tough rule but it kept order in school. I never heard of a kid being sexually abused by a priest. In our neighborhood, most people did not go to the cops, so in Jersey City, sexual abuse of a child would be a death sentence. It was a tough city, but most of the rules made sense.

I loved going to school because it was like a comedy club. We were always thinking of how we could make the class laugh, competing to see who could make the class laugh and who could do the craziest things. Patty would come up with something new everyday; if the teacher gave us a minute alone Patty would have the whole class laughing. Patty would put his thumb through his two fingers as if it was a penis. He started out running around with the thumb between his fingers. Then he put two fingers up on the other hand and started humping it, saying, "Does that feel good, baby?" I don't know how he came up with this stuff. I just could not believe the stuff he invented. He was constant entertainment. Patty did a great James Cagney impression, too: "You dirty rat, you killed my brother." He also liked Gumby and Pokey and he always had Gumby humping Pokey or Pokey humping Gumby. He did an impression of the midgets in the "Wizard of Oz" movie, doing the song and dance routine of the Lollypop Guild and making faces just like the guys in the movie. I loved to hang out with Patty because he was always making me laugh. One of his jokes was to change the words of songs. He changed the harmony of Earth Wind and Fire's "Sing a Song" to "Give me some titties, give me some titties," and he turned, "Hey, Jude by the Beatles" into "Hey, Jude, I saw you nude."

Patty's nutty antics were the only thing that got us through gym class. We didn't really have a gym. We had a basement, and our old gym teacher made us march around and around it. Marching was boring. We did not like boring. Thanks to Patty, whenever we had a boring time, it did not last long. It was like the quiet before the storm; you knew something was going to happen. It was just a matter of time. Patty started singing as if were marching in the army: "If I die on the Russian front, honey, if I die on the Russian front, babe, if I die on the Russian front, I'm going to bury my soul in a Russian cunt," and the rest of us would sing "Honey, honey, babe." The marching in gym class did not last too long because every time the gym teacher made us march, we would start to sing our song.

My favorite gym game was dodge ball. We divided into two teams, and when your team had the big rubber ball, you threw it at the other team. If they caught the ball you were out, and if you hit someone and he didn't catch it, he was out. We were all trying to kill each other with the ball and laughing the whole time we were playing. Dodge ball did not last long though because a couple of children were hit hard in the head with the ball and the principal told the gym teacher we could not play dodge ball any more.

We had to go to the children's 9 o'clock Mass every Sunday. St. Richard's was a beautiful church made of big slabs of stone. The steeple was huge; it looked like a tower and had a clock on the top two sides. The bells rang when it was time to go to church. You could see the tower from most areas of Jersey City. The inside of the church was a work of art. All of the windows were stained glass with beautiful pictures of saints and angels. The walls, floors, and altar were made of marble. Three aisles led up to the altar between the rows of solid mahogany pews. I always went to church with my mother. She had a strong faith in God and did not miss Mass. Most people I knew were Catholic; only a handful were not. I had an uncle that was Protestant but he never went to church. I asked my mother how Uncle Jimmy could be a Protestant if he didn't go to church and she said he was just born that way.

If you did not go to the 9 o'clock Mass the nuns knew you were missing and they would give you a hard time Monday in school. I did not get a lot out of church when I was young. I do not know if they spoke Latin or English, but either way I did not understand most of what they were saying. I said my prayers and then I headed for dreamland. Whenever I found something boring I would go in my own little world, daydreaming about something exiting like beauty contests. My favorite part of Mass was when the girls would go to receive Communion. I would have a little beauty contest in my head. We had to wear nice clothes to church and all of the girls were always dressed in nice dresses. I judged each of them as they passed me to receive Communion, ranking them as "she is a babe," "I would marry her," or "I would need a few beers." I was a little fat kid and none of these girls would have looked twice at me, but it was nice dreaming. If the girl was good looking, I would start singing, "Here she comes the girl of my dreams," and after she received Communion I would say, "Okay, now, turn around so can I get a better look at you, sweetie." I got whacked in the back of the head a lot by the nuns when my singing became too loud. As I got older, I thought most of the girls were pretty. As soon as they started to grow boobs, they at least received the babe vote. The older boys would tell me to be nice to the ugly girls because they could turn into beauties when they got older. They told me, "If you are nice to them now, they will remember you being nice when they are older." Those guys were usually right.

Most of the boys in my class became altar boys. Serving Mass with Patty was always dangerous. If you looked at him while the priest was looking at you, he would make you laugh in the priest's face. One time we were serving a funeral, and Patty made Mickey laugh so hard he dumped the incense all over the altar. I did not like to laugh at funerals because I would have kicked somebody's butt if they laughed at a funeral for one of my relatives. I was always afraid at funerals because you had to think about the dead person. I thought about the accomplishments of the person who died and the things I wanted to accomplish in my life before I died. I prayed that the person made it to heaven. Patty laughed when he was scared or nervous, and if he started laughing, everyone around him laughed, too. The hardest part of the Mass with Patty was when you held the water to let the priest wash his hands because the priest was facing you and Patty was making all kinds of faces trying to make you laugh. I always said Patty would die for a laugh. The priests treated us altar boys special, taking us to the movies and out to eat pizza or hamburgers.

One day after school, Patty pushed one of the teachers down a flight of stairs. The teacher lined the kids up from short to tall and since Patty was the shortest kid in the class, he was at the front of the line. The kids behind him were pushing him, and he pushed the teacher. All the kids laughed when she tumbled down the stairs, but I felt bad for the teacher. She was crying, but she was not seriously injured. I knew Patty did not mean to do it because he didn't laugh or bragging about it. He said, "Hey, Tony, they pushed me into her; I tried to grab her but she was already on her way down the stairs." Kids tried to joke about it but Patty always said, "I tried to grab her." They took him out of our class and put him into a new class because he was making us laugh too much. Class was boring without Patty, but I met him after school to share some laughs.

When baseball season came, I played back-up catcher for Little League, and I had to wear a cup. I had to serve Mass and then go to a Little League game, so I put my protection cup and uniform on and went to church. I put my altar gown over my uniform and went to serve Mass with the priest. I always got a bored in church so I started banging on my cup. First, I started knocking on the cup with one hand and then I started to get a beat so I started knocking on it with two hands. I had a pretty good beat going with both hands; it was like I was playing the bongos. Suddenly I realized what I was doing and snapped out of dreamland. I looked up at the priest. He was saying the sermon but everyone in the church was looking at the kid playing the bongo balls. After Mass, the priest asked me what I had been doing. I told him I had to be a catcher in a baseball game after Mass so I had a cup on and I had to make sure that it worked. Father just looked at me and laughed. He said, "Make sure you protect those jewels!"

Being an altar boy really taught us to be responsible because we had to keep a schedule and make sure we were at the church fifteen minutes before Mass started. We had masses every hour on the hour starting at 6 AM on Sundays, and we had a 6 AM mass and an 8 AM mass on the weekdays. We volunteered to be altar boys for all the Masses. I liked to serve the earlier Masses because the sooner I finished serving Mass, the sooner I could start playing, but the 6 AM mass was too early. Once I did the 6 AM Mass and I fell asleep. I only volunteered for that Mass if no one else did. Being an altar boy was a good job, even though it was sometimes hard. You felt pride because you were serving God. Sometimes an old woman would see you outside the church after Mass and say, "Good job, kid," and that would make you feel even more proud.

When we were not in school, we were out playing all the time. I usually hung out with Chubs, Patty, Chucky, and Mikey. Chucky was a short kid with black hair and he walked with a bounce in his step. Chucky usually had an exciting story to tell you. He was wise for his age, and he was a good friend. Mikey was a taller kid who liked sports and he liked to laugh. We had a lot of friends but if I was going out to play, I would look for them first. I was hardly ever in my house; I usually went out right after I woke up and on the weekends, I only went home to eat and sleep. On the weekdays, we went out to play after school. Our parents did not know what we were doing, but they weren't worried about us. If I stayed in the house too long and I was bothering my mother she would say, "Go outside and play in traffic." She was only kidding, but we went outside. Every day, we played baseball, football, or basketball in the street or a schoolyard. When we were not playing sports, we were getting in trouble.

Chapter Two:

You Better Learn How to Fight

Jersey City was a working class city, and all of our parents worked hard. They didn't have time to give us a lot of day to day guidance, but I think they also knew we had to figure things out for ourselves. I got some advice from my mother, like, when a bully in the schoolyard is messing with you, you have to hit him; after you hit him he will not mess with you anymore. I asked, "What if there are three bullies?" and she said, "Always hit the biggest one or the one with the biggest mouth. After you take him out, the other bullies will be afraid of you." It was easy for my mother to say, but there were a lot of bullies in Jersey City. Most of the people there were tough; they were nice but they were tough. You had to be tough or you did not get any respect. My first fighting lesson came to me on a TV show called "Sunset Strip," a private-eye show. The private eye grabs this person by the tie and punches him. The private eye is beating the crap out of the other person. When his opponent hits the floor, the private eye picks him up by the tie and hits him again. I thought that was the key to winning a fight: you grab the person you are fighting by the tie and punch him. I was six years old and I thought I could do anything I saw on TV.

One nice spring day, I was sitting outside my house on the porch with my mother. She was talking to some neighbors when a fight started between Anthony and Michael, two kids from the block. Both of the kids were trouble-makers. They had just got out of school and still had their Catholic school uniforms on. At first, it was a good fight. Both kids were fighting well; they were trading punches and wrestling a little bit. All of the adults just sat there and watched the fight, no one trying to stop it. It was as if the two kids beating the crap out of each other were entertaining the adults. All of a sudden, Michael started punching Anthony in the face. Anthony's face was full of blood and Michael, pushing him up against the fence in front of his house, was still punching him. It was like watching a boxing match when one fighter has the other fighter in trouble against the ropes. The only problem in street fighting is that there is no referee to stop the fight. I did not know a lot about fighting, but I knew this fight should be stopped. I was looking at the adults, waiting for one of them to stop the fight no one moved. Thank God, Michael's father finally came out of the house and pulled Michael off Anthony. Blood covered Anthony's face and his school uniform. Anthony went home and his parents did not even come out of the house to complain about the fight. My guess is that Anthony's parents told him he had better learn how to fight better. After everything was over all I could think about was that Anthony just got the living crap kick out of him and nobody did anything to help him, but I really did not like Anthony so it did not bother me. I asked my mother why Michael beat up Anthony. She said because he deserved it. She said you always get what you deserve. I asked her if Michael was going to get his butt kicked for what he did, and she said, "Yes, Michael has a butt-kicking coming to him."

"When will it happen?"

"I don't know when it's going to happen," she said. "But I know it *is* going to happen. God always gives you what is coming to you."

All I got out of this is that I better learn how to fight. Nobody helped Anthony, so nobody was going to help me, either. You were all by yourself if someone wanted to fight you. Many kids were always looking for a fight to prove they were tough. If you did not know how to protect yourself, you were going to get your butt kicked.

I had my first fight one day while walking home from first grade. This older kid on my block was always busting my chops. He was walking behind me calling me fat boy. Tommy was not too skinny himself. The fat-boy routine was getting me mad, so I thought I should punch the bully like my mother told me. I watched the private eye show so I knew how to do it. We had just gotten out of school and Tommy had on a tie. He went to St. Richard's also but he was in the third grade, two years older than me so he thought I was afraid of him. He got close to me and said, "Hey, fat boy." I turned around and did not even talk. I grabbed his tie and started punching him in the face. It worked like a charm; I was beating the crap out of him and he had no defense for the tie-grabbing technique. A neighbor woman that lived across the street saw Tommy messing with me every day. She stuck her head out of the window and shouted, "Beat the crap out of him, Tony!"

I must have punched him in the face five times. Then I had him on the ground; I was on top of him banging his head on the ground. My father saw me fighting Tommy and he came running down the street and pulled me off. My father said, "I know that kid deserved to get his butt kicked but I thought you were going to kill him."

The neighbor woman, Mrs. L. yelled, "You should have let him beat him a little more—that kid has been bothering your son every day."

I loved Mrs. L. She was a tough woman, but she was funny. When I got a little older, every time she saw me she would ask, "How old are you now?" I would tell her how old I was, then she would ask me, "Are you still a virgin?" I would start laughing, and she would laugh and hug me.

A few days after my first fight, Tommy wanted to fight me again. He had just finished football practice so he had shoulder pads on. My father said he would have to take off the shoulder pads, but I wanted him to keep them on so I had something to grab so I could hit him. Well, he took them off and fought me without a shirt on. The private-eye lesson did not work because I did not have anything to grab. I got my butt kicked that day. However, the bully never messed with me after that. My mother's advice worked—I hit the bully and then got my butt kicked, but he did not want to fight with me again. It's sad, but being tough was very important. Our parents didn't encourage us to fight but they taught us that when somebody messed with you, you had to be ready to fight. They didn't look down on you if you lost a fight but they would be mad if someone hit you and you did not fight back. My mother told me, "You have to be nice but you have to be tough. It is a tough world and you have to be tough, too."

Chapter Three:

Brooklyn Stories

My mother was from Brooklyn, so while most kids got bedtime stories, my brother John, my sister Karen and I got Brooklyn stories. Brooklyn stories were a lot better than bedtime stories. We heard the same stories over and over but they were good stories so I liked to listen to them. One of them was about the time when my mother and her girlfriends were jumping rope and this man came up to them and said, "Little girls, do you want some candy?" He tried to get them to come into his hallway.

My mother told my grandmother about the man, and my grandmother said, "Next time the man asks you if you want candy, you tell your girlfriends to keep jumping rope and you sneak off and come get me." A few days later, the girls were jumping rope and the man came and asked them if they wanted candy and my mother went off to get my grandmother.

"Mom, the guy is near my girlfriends asking us if we want candy."

Grandma said, "Wait," and she filled this big sock full of coins. My mom and Grandma went around the block where the girls were jumping rope. My mother pointed out the guy and Grandma told my mother to go over by her girlfriends. Grandma went over to the man and said, "Hey, mister, do you have any candy for me?" The man did not know what to say and my grandmother started whacking him in the head with the sock full of coins. She kept hitting him, saying, "Come on, mister, do you have any candy for me?" My grandmother beat the guy up pretty good. Then some construction men that were working on a house in the neighborhood saw my grandmother hitting the guy. They came over and asked, "What's the matter, lady, is this guy bothering you?"

Grandma said, "This guy is trying to get these girls alone in the hallway."

The construction men came down the block and beat the guy up a little more. Then my grandfather and uncles came home from work and asked Grandma what was going on. She said, "This is the guy that was trying to get the girls to go in the hallway with him." My grandfather and uncles beat him until he could barely walk.

My mother said, "The last we saw of the guy, he was wobbling down the street to get away from everyone that was beating him up."

My mother told us many stories like that. I think she was getting us ready for a tough life in Jersey City. The stories were exciting and held a good message. Another one was about a girl she knew. The girl's brother was with a bunch of kids and one of the kids shot a person. The brother was the only one over 18, so he was sentenced to death by the electric chair. He did not even pull the trigger but he had to pay the price for a crime that a younger friend committed. This story taught me that you might get in trouble from being around the wrong people. Another story was about this bad kid that kept robbing stuff. Every time the kid got arrested, his mother went to get him out of jail. Whatever the kid did, his mother never punished him. He kept robbing and his mother kept getting him out of trouble. He finally robbed a bank and killed a security guard. The guy was waiting to go to the electric chair and he called for his mother. She went to see him in jail, and he was all chained up. He said, "Come close, I have a secret to tell you." When she bent over to listen, he bit her ear off. She was screaming, and her son said, "You did not use your ears all of these years—I needed to be punished and you never punished me. Now I'm going to die on the electric chair."

My mother explained, "You have to punish your kids when they do something bad. You love them but you have to punish them so they learn. You can love your kids, but you cannot be their friends all the time. There is a difference between a parent and a friend. A friend will forgive you and tell you it is okay, but a parent has to punish you and teach you a lesson." From her story, I learned that if parents do not punish their kids, the kids will have major problems when they get older. Mom said that most of the kids who are not punished by their parents will end up in jail or will be killed. She always told me if that she would not help me if I got in trouble with police. Protecting yourself is never a crime, she told me, but robbing is a crime.

The stories my mother told me have stayed with me always.

We visited my grandmother in Brooklyn at least once a month. One time I asked my mother why we had to take a two-hour train trip to go to Brooklyn. She said,

"Because I want to teach you it is important to visit your mother when she gets older."

I loved going to my grandmother's house because there were always many people there. My Uncle Robbie and my Aunt Maggie lived with my grandmother in a three-story brownstone. They both liked to drink, but Grandma did not. I loved going to Brooklyn because we always had a good time and I always learned something important.

In the summer, Grandma would turn on the fire pump in front of the house so we could go under the water to cool off from the hot day. On the Fourth of July, Uncle Robbie would buy a lot of fireworks and we would set them off all day and all night. Grandma did not have a lot of schooling but she knew everything there was to know about being a good person. Some people talk about doing good things, but if my grandmother saw something that needed to be done, she would do it. If she saw a bum in the street, she would give him money. My aunts and uncles would tell her the bum was just going to buy booze with the money, and Grandma said, "He needs booze just as you need food." She was a brave woman; she had more guts than most men.

One of my mother's stories was about my grandfather drinking whiskey in a speakeasy during Prohibition, when it was illegal to drink. My grandmother knew if she did not get him out of the speakeasy, my grandfather would spend his paycheck and they would not have money for food. She would let him have a couple of drinks, then she would go down there and get him. One time she knocked on the door of the speakeasy. When a man looked out through the slot in the door, she asked, "Is my husband in there?"

"He's not here," the guy said, but Grandma could see Grandpa through the slot.

She said, "Let me in."

"You can't come in because you're a woman," the guy said.

"If you don't let me in, I am going to call the cops," she said. She knew the neighborhood police knew about the speakeasy, and she knew they would not get my grandfather out of the club, but she said, "Open this door or you'll be sorry!"

The guy laughed at her and closed the peek-through slot on the door. Grandma crossed the street to a vacant lot and picked up a brick. She threw the brick through the storefront window of the speakeasy. When the glass shattered, she walked through the window, ripped down the curtain, grabbed my grandfather by the hair and pulled him out of the speakeasy. As she was leaving, she looked at the guy standing by the front door and said, "I said you would be sorry." My grandmother had the biggest heart in the world but you did not want to mess with her because she was not afraid of anything. Whenever I was with my grandmother and something scary happened she would look at me and say, "Oh, don't worry about it. If you are a good person and believe in God, he will always take care of you."

My grandma owned three apartment buildings and I got to go with her to collect the rent money. The apartments were in the slums but she was not afraid to walk through the slums of Brooklyn to inquire about her rent money. When she had tenants who did not pay the rent, I would say, "Grandma, get rid of them if they are not paying you."

"No, there are more important things in life than money. These people are poor and I have to let them stay here. When you go in front of God to see if he will let you in heaven, he is not going to care about how much money you have. He only cares about how you used your money to do good things." She said, "If I throw these poor people out of their apartments, God is not going to be happy and we do not want that."

My Uncle Robbie had a heart of gold, too; he would give you his last dollar. I saw Uncle Robbie give money to this woman in a store one time because she was looking at food and did not pick up the food. He said, "Do you like that meat?"

She said, "Yes, but I have no money," and he paid for the food. Most people talked about being a good person but I never saw people do good deeds like my uncle and Grandma. Uncle Robbie did what he could to make things better. It seemed like not many grownups did the right thing. They would talk about what was right but they did not buy food for somebody that could not afford it. In school and church, they taught us about feeding the least of our brothers and Jesus saying, "When I was hungry you gave me to eat." The world would be a better place if everyone treated people the way Uncle Robbie did. I wanted to be like him when I grew up.

Uncle Robbie grew up on the streets in Brooklyn and I knew he had the best of teachers in my grandma. Uncle Robbie taught me a lot about how to treat people. When Uncle Robbie took me to a restaurant, he tipped the waiter as soon as he came over to the table. I asked him, "Why don't you wait until after we are done eating to tip the waiter? That is what everyone else does."

He said, "Not everyone is always right. You have to do what works the best. If you want good service, tip them when you walking in and they will take better care of you." We always got our food fast and received excellent service. Uncle Robbie would just wink at me when our food came out first. One time Uncle

Robbie took us to Coney Island. He put my brother John on the bumper car ride. The guy running the ride asked my uncle for a cigarette.

"What kind of cigarettes do you smoke?" my uncle asked. When the guy answered, Uncle Robbie said, "I'll be right back." He bought the guy a pack of cigarettes and a beer. My brother stayed on the ride for three hours and my uncle only paid for one ride. He said, "Most of the time when you take care of people, they take care of you."

My mother was going out one New Year's Eve so she took us to my grandma's house in Brooklyn. When we got there, many of my cousins were there, too. All my aunts and uncles were out of the house, all out at New Year's Eve parties. Grandma told us, "We are going to have a dance contest." My little cousin Karen could dance well and Grandma had a good time watching us. She said, "You want some money?" She never just gave us money because she wanted to teach us that we had to work for money. So when she asked, we all said yes. "Okay," she said. "You have to dance! Shake it up!" We all danced, she smiled, and then she gave us money. "Okay, you can spend half of your money, but you have to save half of it," she said. She had lived through the Depression when they had to be careful with their money. My mother had told me stories about the Depression, saying they didn't get to eat every day. "You do not forget when you go hungry. Therefore, you learn how to save your money because you never want to go hungry again," she said.

The next day was New Year's and my Aunt Maggie was going to make spaghetti. She told my cousin Margaret Ann and me to get dressed. We went to the store with her. It was snowing and Margaret Ann and I threw snowballs at Aunt Maggie. She made the best spaghetti sauce; you could smell it all over the house. She cooked it for hours. First, she cooked sausage and garlic and then she put in the sauce. I could never wait until the sauce was finished cooking. I dipped Italian bread in the sauce, and she said, "You have to wait." In Brooklyn, we played cards and ate a lot. I could not believe how much money the adults bet on the card games. When I was older, my mother told me that most of the women that played cards with Aunt Maggie were wives of guys from the New York mob. Aunt Maggie was married to a guy from the mob. He went to jail and that is all I ever learned about him. Mom said that Grandma had a fight with him because he was bringing stolen stuff in the house.

On the corner of my grandmother's block, a Puerto Rican man had a grocery store. The store had no regular hours; the guy just opened up when he felt like working. I asked, "How can the guy run the store like that."

She said, "Oh, it is not big deal, you look out of your window and if he has the light on you know he is open." It was a tough neighborhood but the people that lived there were nice. My family knew everyone in the neighborhood and my family was respected in the neighborhood. In the summer, people would be partying and you could hear bongo drums. I said, "Mom, it sounds like the jungle."

"What do you mean, *sounds* like the jungle?" she said, laughing at me. "You *are* in the jungle!"

I learned the basics in school and in church but my mother and grandmother showed me how to be a good person. My grandmother told me that when you give the church money or poor people money, God rewarded you. My grandmother did not go to church on Sunday because she had a hard time walking, but she made me go when I stayed with her. I think my grandmother learned everything she could in church, and she practiced what she learned. She had gifts from God because of her good deeds: She had wisdom. She knew what was important. On Christmas, I asked her what she wanted for Christmas. She said, "Do you really want to know?"

I said yes. She said, "I want to get all the homeless people off the street, bring them to my house, feed them, and give them some new clothes."

I said, "Well, I can't do that, Grandma, what about some candy?"

She said, "That will be fine."

My mother told me about one Thanksgiving when my grandmother brought this homeless person home with her. She fed the person and let him watch TV. At night, she let him take a bath. She gave him some of my grandfather's clothes. My mother said after the guy got out of the bath, Aunt Maggie looked at Mom and said, "She is probably going to want us to blow him now." Mom said she was laughing so hard she was crying.

I said, "But Mom, it's dangerous to bring a stranger home like that.

My mother said, "Most people could not do it, but when your grandmother gets a message from God, she does what she is told. But your grandmother would have beaten the crap out of that guy if he had tried something bad."

Grandma did not like my father. She never said anything bad about him, but I knew she did not like him because she was warm and loving to everyone. However, when my father was around her she was serious with him. Grandma thought that my mother deserved a better husband, and my grandma was right. My father went to the bar every day after work to drink. After school, I went to the bar to meet him. I sat at the bar with my father and he would buy me a soda. I did my homework in the bar and the men helped me with it. Dad's habit wasn't unusual in the 1960s. We had three bars on my block and each one of them did good business.

My mother took my brother, sister, and me to a Halloween party at my Aunt Tootsie's house. We had a good time at the party when we were dunking for apples. The adults put blindfolds on us and passed around things for us to feel. "Feel this; it is a cat's eye," they'd say, but I knew it was really an olive. I thought about eating it, but since I could not see it and they said it was a cat's eye, I thought I better not take a chance. The party ended and Aunt Tootsie gave us a lot of candy to take home. It was about a twenty-minute walk home from my aunt's house and it was about 8 o'clock at night. My little brother John was in diapers and my mother was pushing him in the stroller. We got about five blocks from my house when we saw these three kids. One of them had a stick. We passed the three kids and I looked at them. When we got a block away, I told my mother, "I bet those kids were robbing kids' candy sacks."

My mother said, "Don't say that, you don't know they robbed those bags."

One of them had a stick, the other had eight candy bags, and none of them had on customs. We had not walked another block before one of the kids ran on the side of my mother and grabbed the bag out of her hand. My mother started screaming; the kid had to pass us again to get back to his friends. My mother was screaming at the top of her lungs and I did not know what to do because this kid was too big for me to fight. I just watched the kid as my mother was screaming at him. The kid looked scared; he had the look of a halfback that was waiting for a big hit from a lineman in the backfield. He was dancing around so much he looked like he was going to piss his pants. I was kind of hoping the kid would run off because I thought my mother was having a nervous breakdown and even I wanted her to stop yelling. The kid finally passed us and my mother went from screaming to laughing just as hard. I was thinking, *Oh, great, this kid just scared my mother into being a mental case.* Out loud I said, "Ma, are you all right?" She just kept laughing and I asked her, "Why are you laughing?

My mother said, "That kid just stole a bag of your brother's dirty diapers." She said, "He is going to run to his friends, and they are going to say, 'Come on, man, let me see what kind of crap you got in that bag; you got to split this crap up with us. And that is what he stole—a bag of your brother's crap." She said, "They are going to be splitting a bag of crap." She wiped her eyes, still laughing. "I wish I could be there to see their faces when they open up the bag of crap. I told you crime does not pay; all you will get from stealing is crap!" We laughed the whole way home.

Chapter Four:

The Man of the House

When I was nine years old, my mother kicked my father out of the house because he was drinking too much. At the age of nine, I became the man of the house. When my mother told me my father was not going to be living with us any longer, I was heart-broken. It was the toughest situation I had to deal with up to that point in my life. A child does not choose his father, but he loves his father.

It was tough being the man of the house at the age of nine, but I did the best I could. We used to see my father on the weekend. It was not like having a father; it was like having a person you saw on the weekend. Sometimes he would take us to the movies but most of the time we hung out with him in the bar. My father took my sister, brother, and I to the bar and we drank soda and ate chips while Dad drank. He was a chain smoker. He had a station wagon and when it was cold, he would have the windows up and smoke one cigarette after another until the whole thing was filled with smoke. It was like riding in a cloud. I used to like to wait until we started out on a long trip, when I would hide his cigarettes. At first, he thought he lost them and would be looking all over for them. Then he said, "One of you kids hide my cigarettes?" and I started laughing. He pulled the car over and looked over his shoulder at me, sitting in the back seat. He said, "Tell me where the cigarettes are or we are not going anywhere." One time I was in the car with my father and he asked me what I was going to be when I grew up. I said, "I do not know; I might drive a truck."

He said, "Think about it good because once you are eighteen you are on your own."

I thought, *Great, I am only nine and I have to start thinking about a job.* He said, "Once you are eighteen, you are a man and you have to learn how to take care of yourself." I always kept that in the back of my mind and knew I had to be prepared to earn a living when I was eighteen.

My father graduated high school but my mother did not finish it. She dropped out to start working to help her family put food on the table. After my father moved out, I had no one to help me with my homework. My grades got very bad. We pay teachers a lot of money to teach children how to read and write. Our local taxes go to education. There are six hours in a school day, yet the teachers expect the parents to teach the children at home. Some parents are not equipped to teach at home. When there is a problem with a child's education, the teachers blame the parents, the parents blame the teachers, and I say it is just bad planning. If you have children in the classroom for six hours a day and you cannot teach them how to read and write, you should not be a teacher. I would also have the school day match the work day so single mothers can work without having to worry about giving most of their wages to day care. However, we do not plan too much; we just place blame on one another and spend a lot of money on prisons because of poor education. There are great teachers, and we should pay them a lot more, and get rid of the ones that are just collecting a paycheck without doing their jobs.

I was lost in school and doing well in school was not important to me any more. I could not relate to how going to school would help me make money when I got older. My mother used to punish me for getting bad grades but that did not change anything because neither the teachers nor my mother helped me learn. It is sad to say that my father and the guys in the bar were better teachers then the teachers. Once a child gets behind in school, it is hard for him to catch up with his studies. Even when I wanted to learn, I was so lost there was no chance for me to catch up with my schoolwork. I acted as if I knew what was going on in school, but I was lost.

I had to watch my brother and sister a lot when my mother went to church to help with Bingo or went out with her friends. My brother John was a handful. He always gave me a hard time and would not listen to me. One snowy day my mother went to the store to buy food and she told me to watch the kids. My brother was seven years old, he was jumping up and down on the sofa in his underwear, and he was yelling. I told him to calm down but he did not listen to me. I told him if he did not listen to me, I was going to throw him out in the snow. He said, "You are not going to throw me out in the snow in my underwear."

I said, "Keep it up and you will see."

He did not listen to me so I threw him outside the house, locked the door, and looked at him through the window. He was jumping up and down in his underwear and yelling at the top of his lungs. I just wanted to prove a point; I let him back in the house right away, but the neighbor woman looked out of her window and saw the whole thing. She told my mother when she got home, and I was punished for a week—but my brother always listened to me after that.

One day I was downstairs in the basement listening to music. John ran down stairs, crying. He looked scared and I knew he had done something bad. I asked him what was wrong. He told me that he had busted a car window with his BB gun. I told him to get the gun and put it in the basement. I asked him if anyone saw him shoot the window and he said no. I told him to stop crying and not to tell anybody. I told him that if nobody saw him, no one knew he had done it. I said, "Do not tell anybody about this and you will not be caught." Nobody ever found out that he shot out the window.

John was always in trouble. I felt bad because my father was not around and I was the man of the house, but being so young, I could only do so much for my brother. He was left back in the first grade because he hit a kid in the head with a desk. One time this kid came to our door full of blood; he told my mother my brother beat him up. My mother called John and asked him why he beat the kid up. My brother said, "I beat him up because he called you a motherf—." Mom told the kid to get out of there. She never punished my brother for hitting the kid.

Chapter Five:

Excitement in School

When I was in the fifth grade, I asked the teacher if I could be excused to go to the bathroom. When I was walking back to the classroom, I saw my friend Jake and this nun standing outside of their classroom. Jake was in the sixth grade and he lived down the block from me. I knew the nun was tough but I also knew Jake did not take crap from anybody. It was a perfect match up—there was the toughest nun and the toughest kid. I was watching them to see what would happen. I could see Jake's curly, dirty-blond hair over the nun's shoulder. At first, she was just talking to Jake and then all of a sudden I saw her throw a punch at my friend. Jake ducked and the nun punched the marble wall so hard she yelled. Jake just smiled and the nun told him to go back in the classroom. She was shaking her hand in pain. I felt like cheering for Jake but I did not want to make that nun mad because she was crazy. She used to call us the scum of the earth. I saw Jake after school and I said, "Wow, that was something. She would have nailed you with a good punch but you ducked just in time."

He said, "She thinks she is slick but she does not want to mess with me; I am slicker." Jake did not fear anything; he was a tough kid, and he was street smart. I always respected Jake because his had guts.

We were always getting in trouble in school. We shot paper clips, threw balls of clay, and put thump tacks on chairs. One time this girl put a pair of scissors on this fat kid's chair. She could have killed him but, thank God, Harold's fat butt broke the scissors in half. We all knew who had taped the scissors to the chair but nobody said anything. I was watching Harold take his seat and I was afraid the scissors were going to stab into his flesh and he was going to get hurt. When he broke the scissors in half I was so relieved. The whole class was laughing and the teacher asked what happened. This kid said, "Fat Harold sat on the scissors and broke them." The teacher was chuckling and I was just thinking, *I hope we do not see this again.*

One time we were working with compasses for math class. The teacher was teaching us how to draw circles with the compass but after awhile that got a little boring. Therefore, this kid—Adam, but we called him Tex because he was born in Texas—started throwing the compass onto the floor so the sharp point would stick in the hard wood. Every time the teacher faced the blackboard, we threw our compasses to get them to stick in the floor. After awhile that got a little boring, too, so Tex stabbed the kid in front of him in the butt with the compass. The kid jumped up and yelled and Tex was thrown out of school. I felt bad for him, and bad for the rest of us because that was the end of the compass-throwing competitions. I was worried that they were going to throw me out of school also but I did not get in trouble. Tex took it pretty good; he packed up his belongings and left school. I said, "Take care Tex. I am sorry."

He said, "I will be all right, Tony."

Tex had to go public school, and the kids in there thought he was a punk because he came from Catholic school. Two bullies kept bothering Tex, punching him and making fun of him. He was fed up with taking garbage from the bullies so he took the buckshot out of his father's shotgun shells and filled them with salt. The next day the bullies were trying to beat up Tex, so Tex ran to his house and the bullies chased him. Even after he got inside, the bullies were outside yelling at him, so he loaded the shotgun with the shells full of salt. The bullies were knocking on his door calling him a punk, when Tex opened the door with the shotgun in his hand. When the bullies saw the shotgun, they said, "Oh, crap."

Tex said, "They did not look so tough when they saw me run out of my house with the shotgun!" The bullies started running and Tex shot both of them in the legs with the salt. He said, "I was trying to shoot them in the butt but I hit them in the legs." The bullies could not walk for a couple of days and their parents called the cops. They arrested Tex and he had to go to court, where he got probation. It is funny that the adults were not involved when the bullies were bothering Tex; they did not get involved until Tex shot the kids. I was just glad Tex had the sense to use salt and not the real shotgun shells. Tex never got bothered in school again. He did not like being on probation but he felt like he did the right thing. He told me that he had to shot them or they would have bothered him for the rest of his life. "I had to protect myself," he said. I knew Tex was right; if somebody was messing with you, you had to do something to make him stop.

We all had to learn how to protect ourselves; if you did not, somebody messed with you for sure.

One time Patty and I went to church. We sat in the back of the church and Patty was bored so he was trying to make me laugh. He was making faces and dancing in the pew. I did not like laughing in church. No matter what he did, he could not make me laugh. I just ignored him and he stopped trying to make me laugh for a while. I knew it was the calm before the storm because I had never seen Patty sit still for so long before. He was planning his next move. Well, there was this nice nun sitting next to me. She was short and fat and I guessed she was from another parish because we did not know her. When the priest said, "Let us show the sign of peace," Patty looked at me seriously and said, "Peace be with you," and shook my hand. Then he turned to the nun and grabbed her hand and patted her on top of her wimple and said, "Peace be with you, you fat little, chubby little nun." Well, I could not stop laughing. I was rolling around in the pew laughing. The nice nun looked at Patty like he was crazy. I could not stop laughing. I tried to bite my tongue to stop but that did not even work. I had to leave the church. Patty ran outside and said, "Don't you know it is a sin to leave Mass early?" He hugged me and we laughed for a long time.

Once he invited me to eat dinner with his family. He waited until I took a sip of milk then he looked at me with a funny face and said, "Fred Head." I squirted the milk out of my nose. Patty kept my childhood fill of laughter.

In the seventh grade we started going to school dances. They were great—it was like having a license for dry humping. The eighth grade girls volunteered to teach us how to dance, so we met in the school auditorium after school. There was a record player on the stage and as soon as we got in the auditorium a girl grabbed each boy by the hand and Father B put a record on and we started dancing. The girls tried to teach us how to dance fast, which did not hold our interest. After fifteen minutes of fast dancing, they started to teach us how to slow dance. I was in heaven I was dancing with this girl that had a nice body and big boobs, and I had a hard-on that would not quit. The priest stopped the music and said, "Everyone take a seat; I want to tell you something." As I headed back to my seat everyone saw my hard-on. They were all laughing hard, even the priest. I was kind of red in the face but the hard-on didn't quit. I just shrugged my shoulders and sat down as soon as I could. The priest told us we had to dance with rhythm and all I could think was, *Yeah, Father, right, rhythm.* After the priest was finished talking, we went back dancing. I went back to dance with the same girl. I think she liked dancing with me because she pulled me close against her as soon as we started dancing again. All I could think about was how great it was. I could have danced with that girl for a couple of days without stopping.

The school held dances on Friday nights in the auditorium. One night I was slow-dancing with this girl and after the song was over I went to sit down. I was sitting down but I still had a hard-on. This was before they invented Viagra but those hard-ons would last over four hours and I did not need a doctor. My friend's mother came over to ask me to dance with her. I did not know what to do; I had a bulge in my pants and I was not about to get up in front of her with the pup tent action going on. I had to say, "I would love to, ma'am, but my feet are really hurting." I think she got a little upset at me but I just could not explain to her why I could not dance with her. I could just image getting up to dance and her looking at my pants. I did not want to be rude but I did not want to explain the bulge in my pants. I had no control over it; it was not like I was thinking anything bad, it just happened.

Every year St. Richard's Church had a carnival that lasted about a week, with games, some rides, and food stands. The school let us take a half day off on the of Carnival so we could spend our money. Well, Friday came and at 11 AM we ordered food from the Carnival to eat in our classroom. Father came on the loudspeaker and said he needed to meet with all the altar boys in the auditorium. Father said, "Leave your food in the classroom." We had to get ready for a big Mass we were having. Mikey did not listen to Father and bought his pizza and soda with him. He took a big bite of pizza and a drink of his soda, trying to finish it before Father B made him throw the food away. Father started yelling at him. I thought, *Please, Mikey, do not look at Patty.* It all happened so fast. Father was coming up to Mikey yelling, when Mikey looked at Patty, Patty made a face, and Mikey shot pizza and soda out of his mouth all over Father's face. It was like slow motion. We were all laughing so hard we could not stop even though Father was furious. I felt bad for him but I could not stop laughing for about an hour. I was laughing so hard I was crying. The madder Father got, the harder we laughed. He yelled at Mikey a little more, but Father was cool and he forgot about it after awhile. I think we laughed the whole day. Every time I thought about it, I started laughing. I would picture Father yelling and Mikey shooting the food out of his mouth all over the priest. It was so funny that I went home and told my mother, and she laughed just as hard as the rest of us had. That was great about growing up with so much comedy; you could recall things that had happened and just start laughing all over again. I was never bored if I was home because I could just think of something funny that had happened and I'd start laughing. Most of the funny stuff I would share with my mother.

Chapter Six:

Childhood Education

My mother was going out one night so I had to stay home to watch my little brother. We had one sofa in the living room so we would have a fight to see who would lie on the sofa. Whoever was pushed to the floor first had to lie on the floor to watch TV. The person that won got to lie on the couch for the night. Sometimes my brother, sister, and I fought for the couch, but this night it was only my brother and me. It was like a royal rumble. I was bigger than John, but he always gave me a good fight for the sofa—he would wait until I lay down and then he would jump on top of me and shove his big toe up my butt to push me off. This night I won the fight and I was lying on the sofa while John was sitting on the floor watching TV. Back then, we did not have cable so you did not have that many choices on what you were going to watch. My brother was watching "The Graduate"; the movie was somewhat boring so I started to fall asleep. Then Mrs. Robinson started to come on to Dustin Hoffman so I thought, *Let me see this before I go to sleep.* Mrs. Robinson was wearing only a bra; back then we did not get to see that on TV, and if my mother had been home, it would have been turned off. Mrs. Robinson is sitting in a chair with a bra on, Dustin Hoffman is standing behind her, and she takes Dustin's hands and starts rubbing his hands on her breasts. I looked at my brother sitting on the floor to get his reaction to the breast rubbing. His eyes were about to pop out of his head and he started yelling, "Tony, Tony, my dick is growing, my dick is growing!" He asked me if my dick was growing, and I told him, "No, Mrs. Robinson is not doing it for me." I was laughing so hard I was crying. My little brother got his first hard on watching Mrs. Robinson in a bra.

As time went on all of my schoolmates started to hang out together at Thirty-three Schoolyard. Thirty-three School was a public school for developmentally disabled children, only one block away from St. Richard's School. There was a basketball court and a big play area where we could play two-touch football and stick ball. We played basketball, played cards, and learned how to fight. There was always a bunch of kids down Thirty-three Schoolyard, up to sixty kids at one time hanging out. In Jersey City, there was power in numbers and we all stuck together. I learned a lot down in Thirty-three Schoolyard; it was not the perfect education but I know we learned some lessons they do did not teach at school. One of my teachers in Thirty-three Schoolyard was Sonny.

Sonny was a chubby kid full of knowledge. He reminded me of Spanky from the "Our Gang" comedy series. He was from a neighborhood that was controlled by the Mafia and one day we were talking about street fights. Sonny was telling us how they hit this kid with a cedar block and the kid was paralyzed. I hated to hear that the kid got paralyzed. They were fighting just to prove they were hard guys and this kid got paralyzed. I asked Sony why we had to fight all the time. I was happy just playing ball and joking with my friends but the only way of getting out of fights in Jersey City was to stay home. Sony said, "It is like that and we cannot do anything about it. You can be a great fighter but in a street fight somebody could come behind you and hit you with a baseball bat and it is over. I know the fighting is stupid but they have been fighting since the Roman times and they will be fighting after we are dead." I guess he was right but I wished we did not have to fight. There were many crazy kids in Jersey City that did not think about the consequences of fighting. They would kill somebody just to have something to talk about.

Most of fights in Jersey City only involved two people, but sometimes there were gang fights and they were usually very dangerous. One of our friends, Johnny, hit a kid with a bat in a gang fight. He did not kill the kid but the kid was disabled for the rest of his life. Johnny had to go to the youth house, which was jail for kids. Johnny did not learn anything good in the youth house because after being locked up for two years, he got out of jail, and only one day later, he stabbed one of my friends. He was crazy before he went to jail, but after Johnny got out of jail he was so crazy I did not want to be around him for long because when you were around Johnny, something bad was going to happen. Johnny was always nice to me, but I did not get a good feeling around him. Being a little crazy was good in Jersey City; too crazy was not good. Johnny was gunned down in the middle of the day on the streets of Jersey City. This was not a drive-by shooting—the guy had the gun in his hand and was chasing Johnny around the car as he was shooting him. There was a saying in Jersey City: "No matter how tough you are there is somebody tougher than you." That made you think that every tough guy has his day. When you pushed the envelope too much, somebody would take you out. My mother always told me, "You live by the gun, you die by the gun." Johnny was nice in his own way—he just let the street get the best of him. There was still a sweet little kid inside Johnny but the hard guy took over. He got out of control and you could almost see his death coming. I would not call it a death wish, but he had no fear at all.

When I was a child in Jersey City, a fighter or a tough guy got a lot of respect. We all wanted respect and we all wanted to be tough guys. We all tried to look like hard guys; we would wear dungaree jackets or leather jackets and put our collars up. I guess we were going for the Elvis look. We parted our hair in the middle or combed it straight back. A lot of fights got started because somebody wanted something to talk about. There was not a boring day down at Thirty-three Schoolyard because we were always doing something. If we were not playing stickball, football, or basketball we were drinking, playing cards, or just talking. Whatever we were doing, the event was full of excitement. There were many characters the hung out down the schoolyard and everybody had his own act. There were lovers, tough guys, funny guys, thieves, drinkers, and hustlers. We all had a little bit of each in us, but some guys acted on one character more then another. I mainly was humble for the most part and tried to hang low. I loved all my friends. They were not perfect but we all loved each other.

It was great having friends that loved you. We really took care of each other and you could always count on your friends. If you had a problem, they would talk to you. If you got in a fight, they would have your back. The love was so great that you would do anything for your friends. We trusted each other. You find out what your friends are made of when you are getting your butt kicked and you are out-numbered. If a guy stays there and tries to help you and gets his butt kicked, you could count on him. Patty and Chucky were small—they did not weigh over a hundred pounds each—but when there was a fight, they would jump in. Usually they got thrown up in the air, but you knew they tried to help you. Anything I had I would give to my friends and anything they had they would give to me. It was a love that is hard to find.

Most of the kids that hung out at Thirty-three schoolyard were from St. Richard's but some of the public school kids hung out there, too. Whatever questions your parents would not answer, you would get answered by one of the kids that hung out down at the schoolyard. You could talk about anything. If you had a problem you needed to solve or a question about anything, you were not afraid to share it with your friends. We all helped each other whether it was with a fight or helping a family move furniture when they were moving. All of the kids were positive and we kept everything positive. Even when things were down, we always believed things would get better. You could be in a bad jam, like getting ready to get punished by your parents, and would be stressing. Your friends would talk to you and say, "Don't worry about it, it is going to be all right." Moreover, you believed them.

My sister Karen was the smart one of the house. She was no angel, but compared to my brother and me, she looked like she had wings. She was smart in school and knew how to stay out of trouble, for the most part. One day I was in the house with my mother and my sister and her friend were on the front porch. I was eating and my sister came in crying. I looked at her face and she had blood all over her mouth and nose. My mother yelled, "What happened?"

She said, "This kid name David punched me in the face."

My mother looked at me and said, "Go get that kid and kick his butt."

When my mother told you to do something, it was like getting an order from a Don. This kid lived in the projects so I walked up there and saw him riding his bike. I called him and he took off, but I ran in front of the bike and gave him a clothesline with my right arm. I hit him so hard that he did a flip off the bike and landed on the ground. I put my foot on his chest and told him that if he messed with my sister again I was going to kill him. Usually when you kicked somebody's butt in Jersey City, their friends would come looking for you to settle the score. Later that day I heard my sister's girlfriend say that the kids from the projects were going to get me.

I figured I better go up to the projects and get them before they got me. I went down to Thirty-three schoolyard that night and all my friends were hanging out. I told them the kid hit my sister and the kids from the projects were going to jump me. I said, "I have to make the first move." There were about twenty of us and we walked up to the projects, and there were a lot of kids there. One of my friends pointed out a guy named Spider, the leader of their gang. I knew if you get the toughest kid in the gang, the other kids will not fight. The kids from the projects did not think I had the balls to go up there so they were surprised to see me. My friend Greg had this big hunting knife and I said, "Let me borrow that knife for a second." I walked up to Spider and said, "Are you Spider?"

He said, "Yeah; what do you want?"

I pulled out this big hunting knife and told Spider if anyone came looking for me I was going to kill him. I thought his eyes were going to pop out of his head.

I did not want to stab Spider; I just wanted to get my point across. I was afraid he was going to go through a big plate glass window outside of the projects because he was so scared or have a heart attack. Spider said, "Okay, nobody is going to come looking for you from here." I let him go and then he started to say he was going to get us. My friend Anthony jumped on him. Anthony and Spider were fighting and Anthony had Spider on the ground and was punching him in the face. This big fat woman came out of the projects with a pair of scissors and she tried to stab Anthony. Chubs pushed her out of the way. I kicked Spider in the head and we got out of there. I figured I did not want to have a war with big fat ladies with scissors. We never heard from Spider again. That was the last time anyone messed with my sister. You had to handle business like that in those days—it was not civilized. You took care of business or business took care of you.

Chapter Seven:

Recreation

Sometimes we did not have a choice but to get in trouble. If we wanted to play tackle football, we had to go where there was grass but there was not too much grass in the city. We found a place to play but it was the lawn at the Senior Citizen Complex where older people lived, so we had to sneak onto the lawn to play. We would be having a good game and they would call the cops on us. We would jump the fence and run away when the cop car drove up. We would wait a couple of days and go back to play. We could not figure out why these old people were calling the cops on us. We were not bothering them. Maybe they were just grumpy old people that called the cops. After awhile they got use to us playing there and stopped calling the cops. The maintenance man would come out to the field and say, "Listen, when the old ladies complain, you have to leave."

We said, "That's cool; let us know when they complain." Leaving was better than getting chased by the cops. You really learned how to run fast when the cops chased you. We always said that we would treat kids nicer when we became old—if we made it that long.

My friends and I loved to fish but the only place to go fishing in Jersey City was the reservoir. A sign posted there read "Five hundred dollar fine for trespassing." To us that sign meant they had to catch us before we would pay the fine. We cut the fence a little so we could sneak under it; this way we did not have to jump over the fence. We had great times fishing there since no one else would risk the fine; we would always catch many fish. The reservoir was like a resort for us; we would fish and swim in the reservoir and usually no one would bother us. We had a rule that we would clean up after ourselves because the reservoir was not like the rest of the city. It was clean and we wanted to keep it clean. One summer day it was hot and they had fixed the fence where we cut it so we had to jump over the fence to get into the reservoir.

Chubs, Chucky, and I were going to go swimming to cool off on a hot summer's day. I hated jumping the fence; I would always rip my pants or cut my arm. Chucky and Chubs jumped right over the fence but it took my fat butt about ten minutes to get over it. We had just gotten in the water and we were swimming when a cop car started driving around the reservoir towards us. We had never seen cop cars inside the reservoir before. All I could think of was, *I have to move fast.* They had a car and could get to us within minutes, and I had to jump that fence. My fat butt was the first one over. It took me ten minutes to get into the reservoir, but it took me about a second to get out of there. I beat Chubs and Chucky, and they were climbing the fence as the cop car was slowly coming closer. Chubs was laughing as he climbed. "Hey, Tony, your fat butt moves very fast when you are getting away from the cops!" We had to settle for getting wet under the fire pump that day. The cops did not want to catch us because they knew we were only having fun, but we knew we had to take the first get-away as a gift. If we pressed our luck, they would have no choice but to bust us.

We found things to keep us busy when it was hot and when it was cold.

Most kids went sleigh-riding or skiing when it snowed, but we did not have any hills around us so we would make up our own winter sports. When it snowed hard and there was a lot of snow in the street, we would wait on the corner for a car to stop. Once the car stopped, we would sneak up behind it and hold on to the bumper. Once the car took off, we would go for a ride. It was kind of like water skiing. Usually the car could not go too fast because there were five of us on the back of the car. If the car started going too fast, we just let go of the bumper and jumped off into the snow. Sometimes people would jump out of their cars and yell at us, but must people would just give us a ride. I do not know if they did it when they were little or if they just knew we were having fun. Maybe only the cool and wacky people went out in the snow because it was rare that somebody would yell at us. Sometimes they would say, "Be careful back there."

Another sport was hitting cars with snowballs. We would hit them on the side of the car so we did not mess with the vision. Most people would just smile. Sometimes people would give us the finger. Sometimes people would get out of the car to chase us but then we would just bombard them with snowballs and run. Some people would stop and smile. We always stayed busy, even in the winter, but my favorite time of the year was summer.

It was a hot summer day in 1971, and I was eleven years old. Jake, Anthony, and José came to my house to get me. They rang my bell and said, "Get your swimming suit; we are going swimming at Al's house." I got my shorts on and left with my friends. Jake asked me if I knew how to swim, and I said yes. Jake asked José if he knew how to swim. Jose was from Puerto Rico. He said, "In my country we dive off the cliffs into the water. It is very dangerous. If you jump in at the wrong time you will hit the bottom of the rocks and die. If you dive in at the right time and you are not a great swimmer you can drown." We were all impressed with José's story of cliff diving. I was thinking, *Wow José has some balls; I would not dive off the cliff.* We got to Al's house where there was a beautiful above-ground pool with a deck built around it. We were not at the pool two minutes before Anthony pushed José in the pool. José could not swim; we thought he was joking because he was a great cliff diver so we let him go under the water a couple of times. He was yelling, "Help!" but we thought he was joking. When he went down for the third time, we jumped in to save him. José was not a great cliff diver—but he was a great bullshit artist. We were all laughing as José was spitting out water. I learned fast not to bullshit my friends. If you gave them bullshit and got in trouble, they would laugh at you. If you told them the truth, they would help you.

Chapter Eight:

Crime Does Not Pay

We did not have a lot of money. If I wanted money, I had to work for it. Most of my friends were careful with their money. We only paid for things when we had to; we were always trying to sneak into the movies. We would chip in to buy one ticket and one guy would pay. Then he would open the back door for the rest of us waiting outside. Sometimes we got caught and would just run away. Most of the time we got into the movies with the purchase of one ticket. It always felt better watching the movie when it was free. We always rationalize our wrongdoings by saying to each other, "Well, they try to rip us off with expensive popcorn so we have to save on the cost of the movie tickets."

If we went on the trains we would duck under the turnstiles so we did not have to pay the twenty-five cents it cost. We would ride a bus up Kennedy Boulevard; after you got to a certain point you had to pay an extra ten cents. We would never pay the ten cents; we either got off at that point and walked or we waited until the bus driver opened the door and ran. Most of the bus drivers would just let us go but once in awhile the driver chased us. The bus drivers were usually fat and slow so they never gave a good chase. Jake and I were on the bus late one night when we jumped off the bus without paying and this skinny bus driver took off after Jake. Thank God, Jake went first because he was faster than I was and this bus driver was fast. I ran in the opposite direction and hid behind a car. Jake was running fast and the bus driver was right behind him. The bus driver finally gave up and Jake ran down the block. The bus driver got back in the bus. I said, "He almost got you, Jake."

He said, "He was fast—it is a good thing he did not got after you; he would have caught you."

All of this trouble for a dime. We just did not have money so we didn't pay when we could ride free.

I was always looking for ways to make money—shoveling snow, cutting grass, whatever I could do, I did. One time my sister, her friend, and I bought twenty goldfish for a dollar and sold them for a quarter each. We tried lemonade stands, too. There were always businessmen coming home from their jobs in New York City. When they saw us selling lemonade, they would just put a dollar in the cup and say, "I used to do that when I was little, too."

My best money making plan came from selling firecrackers. I was twelve years old. It was not legal, but everyone had firecrackers. I went to China Town in New York and bought a mat of firecrackers for eight bucks and then sold them for a quarter a pack. I made twelve dollars profit per mat. I kept the money in a big piggy bank I had on a desk. My mother said, "You are saving a lot of money!" But that business did not last long. I was at school playing basketball and one of the priests told me the cops were asking about me. I sold this kid a pack of firecrackers and the cops caught him lighting them. The kid told the cops I sold him firecrackers. The priest told me he was not mad at me for selling firecrackers but he would be mad at me if I beat the kid up for telling on me. The priests knew it was common practice for a rat to get beat up. The priest said to me, "Listen, I did not have to tell you they were looking for you; now give the kid a break."

I said, "Okay, Father. I will not hit the kid." As he left, I said, "Hey, Father, thanks for giving me the warning." I was scared the cops were going to send me to jail so I got all the firecrackers out of my house. I prayed every day for two months that the police would not arrest me. They finally made it to my house one rainy day. The doorbell rang and two men wearing black raincoats were there. I knew they were not selling Girl Scout cookies. I answered the door and they said, "Is Anthony home?" For a moment I thought to say no, but I knew that it would not help. I had to take the punishment like a man.

I said, "Yes, I am Anthony." They looked at each other and smiled. They probably were thinking it was some big operation, and here was this little fat kid selling firecrackers. Well, thank God, that helped me. They asked me if my mother was home and I went to get her. My mother and the police officers sat in my living room and asked me if I sold the firecrackers to the kid. I said, "Yes, I did." They asked me where I purchased the firecrackers and I told them I had a couple of packs of firecrackers left from last Fourth of July that my Uncle Robbie gave me. I said this kid saw me shooting off the firecrackers and I sold him a pack for a quarter. I thought my mother was going to have a heart attack. She believed me and the cops believed me. The cops told me if they caught me selling fire-crackers again I was going away. I had to close up shop. It was hard to close such a thriving business but I did not want any part of jail. I did not want to give my mother a heart attack, either.

I gave away all of my fireworks to kids I knew would not rat me out if they were caught. When you are doing illegal business, you have to be careful who is involved; you cannot trust most people that are not your friends. One side of me wanted to beat the living daylights out of the kid that ratted me out to the cops but I had given the priest my word. The other side of me knew the kid was afraid of the cops; he was not a tough kid. When I saw him, I said, "You ratted on me and if it were not for Father Roger, I would beat you up." He said he was sorry and I told him he was a rat and could not be trusted. I had to find a new way to make money.

It was Christmas time and Patty asked me if I wanted to go Christmas shopping. We did not have a lot of money so we were planning to get some five-finger dis-counts. I went to Patty's house and his mother and father were not home, so Patty pulled a bottle of whiskey out of the closet. We took a couple of slugs of whiskey and went shopping. We stole Christmas presents for our whole family. I did not like shoplifting with Patty because the whole time we were stealing stuff he was laughing. Patty would be shoving stuff down his pants and start saying, "Ha, look at this Tony, ha, ha," and I would start laughing but in the back of my mind, I was thinking that Patty was going to get us caught because he was draw-ing attention.

Another time I went to the store with Jake and Patty. Jake looked at me and said, "I have to go to the bathroom." His face was red and he looked like he was going to cry.

I went to the bathroom to see what was wrong with him and he said, "I robbed this fishing lure and put it down my pants and it hooked my nuts. Oh, crap, the hook cut into my nuts."

I said, "Shoving hooks down your nuts is not too smart, Jake."

He said, "Yeah, I know but I thought since it was still in the package the lure would not catch my nuts." He put the fishing lure back and said, "I would rather have my nuts than the lure."

In the wintertime, I wore my father's army coat. It had huge pockets and I would fill up the pockets with stuff. Sometimes we changed the price on what we wanted. If a fishing lure was three-ninety-nine, we would find something that had a price of ninety-nine cents and switch the prices. Changing prices was better than putting things in you pocket because you could talk your way out of the price changing, but if they caught you with their merchandise in your pants, you were going to jail. Sometimes when we got up to the counter, the person at the register would say, "This is not ninety-nine cents."

Then we would say, "Oh, it was marked ninety-nine cents; how much is it?". They would say, "It is three-ninety-nine."

"Oh, that is too expensive," we would say. "Please put it back."

We always had this saying when robbing "Don't get greedy—when you get greedy you get caught."

Jake had a lot of experience robbing; he was a master at robbing freight trains. They called robbing trains hitting the freights and it was exciting and dangerous.

Jake loved action. I never had a boring time with Jake. Every day was action-packed. Jake stole beer, calculators, shoes, Spam, and car tires from the freight trains. As much as Jake stole, he never made any money because the cops would always find where he hid the stuff he took. If the cops did not find the stuff, somebody else usually ripped him off. I always listened to Jake and he would tell me how he got ripped off. I started to think it was God's way of letting him know that crime did not pay. At first, I thought it might just be a coincidence but after awhile I knew it was true that when you robbed somebody, somebody else robbed you. I had always heard that what goes around, comes around and it all started to make sense. Jake and I never got caught shoplifting. We were careful and if somebody was near us, we knew it was the store security people and we would not take anything until they left. I almost got caught stealing once when I was in the store with my father. I wanted to steal these football pads for my hands but this guy was next to me and would not go away. Thank God, I did not take the pad because when we were leaving the store I saw that guy in the store's security office. My father would have killed me if he knew I was shoplifting.

Patty got caught stealing a hat with Murray, this chubby redheaded kid. Patty made Murray put this hat down his pants. Murray was walking out of the store and he looked like he had these huge balls. Patty was laughing in the store, saying, "Hey, Murray your nuts swelled up a bit." They got caught while they were walking out of the store. Security busted the two of them. Patty's mother had to go to the store and pay for the hat.

I always felt bad about robbing. I was talking to my friend Sonny about it down the schoolyard, and he said, "Listen, I was talking to Father about robbing and he said God is really going to punish you if you rob from an old lady, but if you rob from a big store, well, they got more then you so they should share with us." It seemed like every time we robbed something, somebody robbed us. One time Jake robbed a freight train and got calculators. This guy told Jake he wanted to buy the calculators; the guy ripped Jake off. That seemed to happen every time we stole something. God was sending us a message. After awhile I just figured out. The Ten Commandments say not to steal, so since there is nothing in the Commandments about a point system between robbing from old ladies and big stores, I was not going to steal anymore. I have had a lot of thing stolen from me in my life. Every time I am ripped off, I know it is God paying me back. I do not get mad, I just hope the people learn from their mistakes. Whatever you do in your life, it will come back to you. I learned it was better if I did good things.

We were bad kids but we did have a good side to us. We helped people if they needed help. We would help older people with groceries. I picked a woman up once that slipped in the snow and walked her all the way home because she was afraid to walk in the snow alone. Poor old woman kept telling me she wanted me to meet Freddy. I am thinking, *Why the hell ain't Freddy driving you to the store?* We got to her house and Freddy was a bird; the poor woman lived with a parakeet. The only love she had in her life came from a parakeet. While I was walking with her, I was thinking, *Why are they letting this woman walk alone in the snow?* It was sad to see her live alone. I always wanted a big family so I did not have to live alone.

Chapter Nine:

Drinking

The first time we went drinking, I was in the seventh grade. It was a cool fall night and we were just sitting around talking, not doing anything. Stanley said, "Hey, guys, what are we going to do tonight?" He said, "Why don't we buy some booze and go drinking?" I never drank before and did not have any desire to drink, but I did not want my friends to think I was a punk so I just went along with the crew. Stanley passed around a hat and said, "Put your money in for the booze." When he had collected all our money, he said, "Okay, now who is going to buy the wine?"

We went to the liquor store and there was a hitchhiker outside of the store. He was not having much luck getting a ride. Anthony said, "Give me the money." Anthony walked over the hitchhiker and told the guy he would pay his bus fare if he bought us wine. We bought eight bottles of wine, took it to the reservoir, and jumped the fence. It was dark and nobody could see us drinking there, but I was afraid to get drunk so every time they passed me the bottle I put my tongue on top of the bottle and turned the bottle up so I did not drink much but it looked like I was drinking a lot. Every time they gave me the bottle Stanley yelled, "Go, go, go!" He said to the other guys, "Tony knows how to drink." One of the kids puked on his new jacket. Drinking was a big show to impress your friends; I did not need to drink because I had fun with my friends without drinking.

As time went on, drinking became a regular event especially on Friday and Saturday night. All of my friends drank on the weekend. When I was younger, I always said I would never drink when I got older. I wish I had kept the promise to myself; nothing ever good came out of drinking.

It was Friday night and I went to Jake's house to get him. Jake only lived one block away from me. He asked me if I ate, I said yes, and he said, "I have to get something to eat before I start drinking." So we went to White Castle and he bought some hamburgers and fries. He paid for it but when he looked for the fries, they were not in the bag.

He asked the woman at the counter for them and she said, "I gave them to the guy who just left." So Jake ran outside and the guy was already in his car. Jake ran up to the car and knocked on the car window. He said, 'Give me my fries."

The guy said, "No, get the hell out of here," so Jake punched him in the face. The guy jumped out of his car and chased Jake with a belt but he could not catch him. I sat in White Castle and watched this grown man chasing Jake up and down the street. I was thinking, *Jake is nuts. The woman at White Castle should give him the fries because she messed up the order and gave them to the wrong person.*

Jake came back in and said, "That guy was kind of tough." He went back to the counter and said, "Listen, woman, the guy would not give me my fries." The woman gave him an order of French Fries. When he finished eating he turned to me and said, "Do you have any money?"

I said, "I have a couple of bucks."

He said, "Okay, buy a bag of ice. We are going drinking tonight."

Jake had robbed a train and he had a case of scotch. He said, "We have a little bar at the pig farm." The pig farm was in back of a factory next to the highway, and nobody bothered us there most of the time. We called it the pig farm because it was dirty. We usually hung out in places that had at least three escape routes in case we got rousted by the cops. The best escape from the pig farm was a highway that ran above it.

When me and Jake got down to the pig farm, Stanley, Mikey, Anthony, and Chubs were already drinking. They had a bar set up with soda, a case of Scotch, plastic cups, and ice. I drank some Scotch, and I was beginning to feel it pretty strongly when the cops came and we ran. Jake said, "The cops won't chase us; they just want the Scotch," so I headed for the highway and got away. I went to hang out at Thirty-three schoolyard, and it felt like there was an earthquake and the ground was moving all night. When I went home, my mother asked me what was wrong with me and I told her I got hit in the head with a basketball. I did not feel good so I went to sleep as soon as I got in the house. It was the first time I had ever gotten drunk.

Chucky and I were playing cards down the schoolyard one Friday night and drinking malt liquor. I drank two six-packs of malt liquor and got ripped. We went to Chuck's cousin's house, about a thirty-minute walk from my house. When I left after awhile, I was so drunk I started walking home the wrong way. I was already late; I had to be home by 10 PM. I met a big biker dude who was hitchhiking, and I asked him for a cigarette. As I lit up, I said, "Can I hitch with you?"

"Where are you going?"

"Jersey City," I said.

"Man, you're going the wrong way!"

I had to hitch the other direction by myself, but finally someone picked me up in a green station wagon. The guy seemed kind of weird; he stopped for a six-pack even though I told him I needed to get home right away. He asked me if I wanted a beer, and I said, "No. I am already drunk and I am late." I told the guy, "My mother is going to kill me." At last he dropped me off down the block from my house. I got home about an hour late. I went in the house and started to wash my face, and my mother saw that I was drunk. She started checking my arms for needle marks. I was so drunk she must have thought I was shooting up drugs, too. My mother punished me for a week, but it didn't take. I was not allowed to leave the house, but the day my punishment was over, I bought a quart of beer. From then on, if I had been drinking, I went right to bed as soon as I got home so my mother would not see me, but she knew. She never punished me for drinking again; she just said I smelt like wine when I came home. She said, "One day you and your friends down in that schoolyard are going to get in trouble."

I found out weeks later that the man who had given me the ride while I was hitching was a child molester. My mother was reading the newspaper and I saw the man's picture by the article. She said he used to molest kids and somebody took care of him; they found him dead by the train tracks. God had to be protecting me because he did not try to molest me.

Patty got so drunk one night on vodka that he was puking all over the place. He could hardly walk. We tried to get him sober and made him drink coffee but he kept throwing up. We carried him to his house, propped him up by the front door, rang his doorbell, and took off. His mother came to the door and said, "What is wrong with you, Patty." He told his mother a bum stuck a needle in his arm, and his parents rushed him to the hospital. They ran into the emergency room and told the nurse that he'd been stuck with a needle. The doctor smelled his breath and told Patty's parents that he had been drinking and did not have any needle marks. The doctor had to pump his stomach. Patty had finished off a whole pint of vodka and got alcohol poisoning. We got so we didn't drink hard alcohol; we just drank beer. If it was cold out, we drank brandy to warm us up.

We usually had the older kids from Thirty-three schoolyard buy our beer for us but one night the older kids went some where and we did not have anybody to buy our beer. This kid Steven that hung out with us was a little slow. Patty said, "I got an idea. I am going to write a note and tell the bartender that Steven's mom is sick in bed and she wants Steven to bring a case of beer home for her." I was thinking, *Patty is nuts; this is not going to work.* But he found this old crumbled-up piece of paper and wrote a note: I am sick and cannot get out of bed; please give my son a case of beer, thank you. Patty signed the note "Mrs. Smith." We waited across the street, hiding behind a car as we watched Steven go into the bar with the note; we were laughing our butts off. I said, "Patty this is not going to work."

Patty was laughing. He said, "Let's see what happens."

I was waiting to see Steven get thrown out by the bartender, but he came out of the bar with the case of beer and a big smile. We were all on the ground rolling. We asked Steven what the bartender said. He said, "He said, 'Tell your mother this is the last time I give you beer.'" I guess the bartender thought if he were sick in bed, he would want someone to bring him a case of beer, too.

Now you might be thinking what bad kids we were. However, we were just imitating our parents. All of our parents drank and most of them smoked. We were just trying to be like them. We all thought it couldn't be that bad if they did it. Drinking became our main hobby. Whatever we did, we started drinking before we went anywhere. If we went to a dance, we drank. If we were going to have a street fight, we drank. If we went to see a sporting event, we drank. If I did not drink on Friday and Saturday nights, I was mad and thought I had missed something. One Friday night I feel asleep on the sofa and did not get up all night. The next morning I was mad because I missed the action of Friday night. I was sitting on the sofa and my sister came in the living room and said to me, "Oh, Tony you are nuts."

I said, "What did I do?" I figured I could not have done anything wrong in my sleep.

She said, "Last night I was watching TV with Mommy in the living room. You were sleeping on the sofa, and in the middle of your sleep you sat up and said where is the beer and went back to sleep." She said, "Mommy got mad." Even in my sleep, I was thinking about beer.

By the time we were fourteen years old, we were hanging out in bars to do our drinking. When it was cold, we would look in this bar where an old guy named Chucky tended bar. If he was working, he'd let us in and serve us. He said, "Listen, I know you guys are not eighteen, so if the cops or the owner comes in just leave." He said, "I know it is cold outside."

It felt good sitting at the bar; you felt like a grown-up. Most of our parents drank. My father drank every day of his life. I always thought a problem drinker was a guy that drank at night and would not get up and go to work the next day. If you got up and went to work, you did not have a problem.

I was wrong.

Chapter Ten:

Sex Education

We were all down the schoolyard and Stanley was telling Patty how to whack off. He said, "Patty, it is great, you have to try it."

Patty said, "As soon as I get home I am going to give it a whack, ha, ha." Stanley started laughing. The next day he asked, "So, did you try it?"

Patty said, "Oh, yeah, I did it, it was great."

Stanley said, "What happened?"

Patty said, "I did it in my bathroom and it hit the ceiling, it went all over the wall, I almost flooded out the bathroom. I started making these weird sounds and my mother was knocking on the door saying, 'Patty, what are you doing in there?' I said, 'Oh, I am fine, Mom, I will be right out of the bathroom."

We were all laughing so hard listening to Patty tell us the story we started crying. Stanley was a bad kid but I loved him because he was always doing something that would make me laugh. Stanley was the type of kid that jumped on you, got you down on the ground, and started giving you titty twisters. He laughed the whole time he was twisting your titties. You wanted to kill him but you could not because you were laughing your butt off.

I was only nine years old when I met Stanley for the first time. He did not go to St. Richard's; he went to public school. Stanley lived around the corner from Chubs and they were friends.

A local restaurant called Chicken Delight delivered to our neighborhood, and Stanley used to call them up to order chicken. He'd give them an address, then call back and order chicken to another address. When the delivery driver came to the first house, Stanley opened the back door of the delivery car and stole the chicken going to the next place. He'd sit there eating his chicken and singing the restaurant's TV jingle: "Don't cook tonight—call chicken delight." I could not believe it. Stanley was only about ten years old and he was robbing Chicken Delight.

Stanley had big brothers and one of them was in this gang called the Bishops. Stanley was always in trouble; I did not hang out with him every day, but when I did, he was always doing something crazy.

Chapter Eleven:

Hanging Out Down the Schoolyard

We were down at Thirty-three Schoolyard one day right after Christmas and it was cold. We were freezing but we did not want to go home, so we got a dry Christmas tree that somebody had put in front of their house for the garbage men to take. We put some lighter fluid on the tree and Tex threw a match to set the tree on fire. We sat around the fire singing songs. It was just like a little campfire and we were keeping warm. We stayed warm for about two hours—then the fire truck came with the cops. They tried to catch us but we had so many ways to escape they did not have a chance, plus it was more important to put out the fire than it was to catch us. No matter how cold it was, we were hanging out every night at the schoolyard.

One time they resurfacing the road down on Kennedy Boulevard right above the schoolyard. They left the keys in this big tar roller, and one of the kids from the schoolyard had to see if he could drive it. Roger started the roller but he could not find the brake; he jumped off and the roller went right into this new car lot. It hit this new car and kept rolling—we all took of running.

We were playing basketball when the cops zoomed into the car lot and turned off the roller. We went over and asked them what had happened. They were laughing as they asked, "Did you little brats start this roller?"

We said, "We do not know how to drive a roller!"

The cop said, "I can see that!" They grabbed us but we kept saying we did not know anything about it. They asked us if we had seen anyone driving the roller and we said no, we were playing basketball.

Thirty-three Schoolyard could turn from a sports arena to a very violent place, fast. One night this kid Dave was teasing this girl. He kept making fun of her. She said, "If you do not stop bothering me I am going to get my big brother and he is going to kick your butt." He kept messing with her so she left. About a half hour later, a car came speeding into the schoolyard. These three guys jumped out of the car. I knew them, and all of them were crazy. They lived down the block from my house, across from Jake's house. Chester was the girl's brother and he had a huge triangle knife, like the kind of knife you would see in a horror movie. I saw Chester whip the knife out and my heart started beating fast. All I could think off was, *Crap I hope Dave can run fast,* because I knew Chester would stab him if he caught him. Chester chased Dave around this car and said, "If you bother my sister again, I am going to come back and kill you." Dave took off running and they did not catch him, but he never messed with that girl again. Chester wanted to get a point across, and he knew he did not have to stab Dave to get him to stop messing with his sister. In Jersey City, it was nice to have an older crazy brother that would protect you. Crazy people got a reputation and people knew if you messed with their friends or family they were going to pay.

Down the schoolyard, we always told stories about street fights. We heard stories of crazy people that were legends in Jersey City. One guy, Sun, lived in a neighborhood that the Mafia controlled. I never saw him, but Sonny knew him. One time Sun beat up three cops. They said one of the cops shot him in the stomach and he beat the cops with a bullet in his stomach. There was another legend name Stone. They called him Stone because he had a metal plate in his head after being hit in the head with a big stone. In a street fight, he would beat up five guys at one time. We argued over who would win a fight between Stone and Sun. It was as if we had our own superhero action figures. Another legend was Screwy Louie. Louie's brother was killed by the mob. They found him with a bullet in his head, tossed in a car trunk in the junkyard. Louie always had a gun. They said during a street fight this kid called out Louie and took his belt off started twirling it around. He said to Louie, "Come on, I am going to kick your butt." They said Louie started laughing at him; Louie pulled out his gun and shot the guy in the leg. Louie is the only legend I met in person.

He was around seventeen years old and drove a black Cadillac. That car was beautiful—it had a chrome plate in the front and big whitewall tires. He was a little guy, short and skinny, with combed back jet-black hair. He wore a pressed jean jacket with the collar up, a white shirt, and a pair of black pants. Louie was cool; he had no fear at all. He was the type of guy who had no fear of death. You would rather get in a fight with a big bouncer than with Louie because even if you beat him, he would come back and shoot you. One day we were hanging out in the schoolyard and Louie was sitting with us on the steps. It had just finished raining and I had an folded umbrella in my hand.

Louie was telling us about the first gun he ever owned. In the middle of Louie's story, a cop car pulled into the schoolyard. Louie saw the cops coming and said, "Not again. They mess with me every day." Even the cops knew Louie was a legend because they pulled into the schoolyard and went right over to search him. The cops did not search us—only Louie.

The cops put him up against his car and said, "Okay, Louie, you know the routine." They made him spread-eagle and they patted him down. When they did not find anything on Louie, they said, "Take care, Louie, we will see you again very soon."

When they left, Louie said to me, "Look in your umbrella." I opened it and found a bag of weed in there. He said, "I would have told the cops it was mine if you got caught, but I know they only search me." We asked Louie where the gun was, and he said, "In my trunk. They usually do not search the trunk of the car." He said, "I used to carry the gun, but I am searched at least once a night. There is some law that says they cannot search your car unless they catch you breaking the law."

Some guys in a silver Cadillac drove into the school yard looking for Louie. One of the guys said, "Louie, we need to talk to you."

He said, "I have to go, fellows," and he drove off. I never saw Louie again after that night.

One hot summer night we were playing two-touch football in Thirty-three Schoolyard when this kid with long hair and a bandanna around his head came in the schoolyard. He pulled out a pearl-handled pistol, and I almost crapped my pants. It's funny; when a gun gets pulled, you start thinking a million things at once. I think God gives us a blood rush because he knows it might be our last thoughts. The guy pointed his gun at my friend Mat. Mat had been bothering this smaller kid, Joey, and Joey had told Mat he was going to call his cousin from New York to take care of him. Turns out, this guy with the pearl-handled pistol was Joey's cousin. He said, "If you don't stop messing with my cousin, I am going to kill you. The next time I have to come back to Jersey, I am going to kill you."

You want to help your friend, but when someone has a gun and you don't, all you can do is pray. Joey's cousin put on a nice hard-guy show and scared us out of our pants. I was impressed with Mattie, too; he took it good. I did not like guns because there were too many hot heads in Jersey City; just a squeeze of the trigger and someone could be killed. Joey did not hang out with us after that; we did not take care of our problems that way. My mother always said, "Live by the gun, die by the gun." If you messed with the wrong people in Jersey City, you could wind up dead. Even though we didn't carry guns, all of my friends acted like hard guys in Jersey City—it was a defense mechanism.

About a year after Joey stopped hanging out with us we learned he was shot to death in a gang fight. His cousin was stabbed to death in a different gang fight. You could act tough but if you went around pulling guns on people, somebody was going to kill you. I really liked Joey when we were alone; he was like a little kid. He had a good heart. I wish it could have turned out differently for him but the Bible says live by the sword, die by the sword. Joey did both.

The two toughest kids from Thirty-three Schoolyard were Jake and Anthony. Everyone down Thirty-three Schoolyard acted like a hard guy, but Jake and Anthony were real tough guys. Both of them loved to fight, and Jake would fight anybody. If he was in a fight, he would win, too. There were many hard guys in Jersey City. If somebody messed with Jake, he would fight them. It did not matter who you were, a kid or a man, if you messed with Jake, you had a fight on your hands. Anthony was a good street fighter, and I wish he would have turned into a pro fighter. I think he would have been a champ. If you went somewhere with Anthony you knew there was going to be a fight. I saw him in a lot of tough fights, and Anthony could hold his own with anybody. I saw him fight grown men when he was sixteen years old. Anthony fought one guy in a gas station until both of them were full of blood. Neither Anthony nor the other guy would give up. After about twenty minutes of them battling back and forth Anthony said, "Did you get enough?"

And the man said, "Did you get enough?"

Anthony said, "Yeah."

He never had hard feelings after a fight; it was like a sport. Both Anthony and Jake had balls; balls were good in Jersey City and if you had brains to go with them, you could go a long way. Without the brains, the balls could get you killed. Anthony finished a lot of fights that other kids started. If you had trouble with somebody, you would go to Anthony or Jake and they would help you. If we got into a street fight, it was usually Jake or Anthony who would throw the first punch.

The first big street fight we got into started at a St. Richard's Carnival. The street fight got started over a girl. I was singing with my class on the stage of the auditorium in the school when this big fight broke out and the whole auditorium got cleared out. We had to finish our song without an audience. As soon as we were done singing, Chubs, Chucky, and I ran outside to see what had happened. Anthony's girl friend had been kissing this other guy so Anthony punched the guy in the face. The other guy was not from our neighborhood; he was from Mosquito Park in Jersey City. That was the first time I found out how important numbers of people are. There were about fifty of us and the guys from Mosquito Park got their butts kicked. It was the start of problems between us and the guys from Mosquito Park. I liked all of them, but I had to fight for my friends. The street fighting got crazy. If they caught us, they would try beat us up, and if we caught them, we would beat them up. I did not like always having to watching my back. One day after school, we went down to Thirty-three Schoolyard to play basketball and found that all of our basketball baskets were ripped out of the ground. The guys from Mosquito Park had brought a truck into our schoolyard, tied a chain around the base of the pole, and ripped the hoops right out of the ground. That really got us mad.

Since we could not play basketball, we started to plan our attack. Jake got an idea and started plotting our revenge. "We have to get them back. We cannot let them get away with this," he said. "They messed up our schoolyard, let's mess up their park." He said, "Tomorrow we are going to buy gasoline and make Molotov cocktails and burn down their park."

We did a lot of crazy stuff but this was getting too crazy for me. I did not want to kill anybody. The next night, they filled up bottles with gas and put rags in the top of the bottles and bombed Mosquito Park with those Molotov cocktails. I stayed home that night. I did not have a warm feeling about Jake's plan. We had to lay low for a while after that, but the boys from Mosquito Park never messed with our basketball hoops again.

We called the night before Halloween mischief night. On mischief night, we would throw eggs and hit each other with socks full of flour that left white marks on our clothes. I was hanging out in the front of my house with my friend Moon. My mother was out and I was keeping an eye on my sister and brother. My brother came in the house and told me this big kid had stolen his eggs. I went outside to see who was messing with my brother, and I told the kid he had better give my brother back the eggs. He told me he was going to kick my butt, and I told him if he kicked my butt he would have problems with the boys from Thirty-three schoolyard. He said he knew them and they were not going to fight with him. The kid and I started fighting; we were rolling around on the floor wrestling when Moon hit him over the head with a soda bottle. The top of the bottle split in half and there was glass everywhere. The kid put the top of the bottle around his finger and cut my face just above my nose. I was bleeding everywhere but it looked worse then it was. I told my brother to run down the schoolyard to get Jake. The kid took off. John ran down the schoolyard but Jake said, "Tell your brother to come down here." When I got down the schoolyard and my friends saw my face covered with blood, they went nuts. We all went up by my house. I had to go in the house because the cops were there. I told them I slipped and cut myself. Meanwhile, my friends caught up with the kid by Journal Square. Jake jumped on him and was punching him while Timmy kicked the kid in the head with boots on. Jake grabbed the kid by the collar and lifted him up, but the kid did not move. Jake looked at Timmy and said, "Oh, great, you killed the kid." They all ran and left the kid laying on the floor. Thank God, the kid only got knocked out. I think he had some medical bills and his mother was calling my mother to find out who did it, but I told my mother, "We don't know nothing," and that is the way it stayed.

Chapter Twelve:

Mulligan's Lounge

Timmy did not usually get into fights but he was a good friend of mine and he thought that kid had to pay for what he did to me. Timmy was a smart kid who always did well in school. Most of us did not do so well. Most of my friends that had gone to public school had to go back to get their GEDs because they just went to school to drink beer, but not Timmy. He did his schoolwork and after school he had a job. One day I was hanging out with Timmy by Mulligan's Lounge and there was a bunch of guys drinking on the corner. A lot of tough guys hung out at Mulligan 's Lounge.

Timmy looked at me and said, "I am getting out of here when I get older."

I was amazed. I said, "You can't leave here! This is all we know and all we have!"

Timmy just looked at me and said, "These guys are going too be doing the same crap when they are thirty years old and there is more to life then getting drunk every day." I knew Timmy was making his plan to leave when he got older and it got me thinking that I could get away from the city if I wanted to.

We were hanging outside Mulligan's Lounge one summer afternoon, just talking. We had just got done playing baseball and we had our bats and gloves. Two older guys, Smitty and Freddie, left the bar. Both of them were nuts. Later, Smitty got shot with a shotgun and lived. They were crossing the street and this speeding car almost hit them. Smitty yelled, "Give me the bat, Anthony!" Anthony threw him the bat and Smitty chased the car until it stopped for a red light. He ran up to it and started to pound the car with the baseball bat. One of the guys inside the car yelled, "Get the gun."

Freddie yelled, "Get the gun and I will shove it up your butt!" They banged up the car and broke all of the windows. It was funny back then; the cops never came. Years later, I saw Freddie on the TV show "Cops." He was a detective that raided a drug house—oh, how the world turns. Smitty was not so lucky. He left the city, moving down to Key West and opening a motorcycle shop; he was doing well for himself. He should have never come back home. On a visit back to Jersey City, he overdosed on drugs. They found him dead in an abandoned building in New York City, a needle stuck in his arm and a bag of heroin by his side.

Mr. Mulligan owned Mulligan 's bar, a nice little neighborhood place on the block where Chubs and Anthony lived. He was always good to us. The bar was usually packed all day long, but there were not many fights there. People respected Mr. Mulligan and if there was a problem around the bar, they knew to take it somewhere else. Most people that went there were from the neighborhood so they were all friends. Mr. Mulligan sponsored softball teams and always took the time to talk to the kids. You knew Mr. Mulligan was a special kind of guy. I always felt good when I talked with him. He was the kind of person who would do something for you and never tell anybody what he did. He always marched in the St. Patrick's Day Parade, and one year he was named Irishman of the Year in Jersey City. He wore a black suit with a green cloth draped across his body. Mr. Mulligan was a Marine and a war veteran. He knew everybody in Jersey City. Mr. Mulligan was friends with the police and the criminals and he treated them all with respect.

It was a hot afternoon and Chubs, Anthony, and I were hanging out on the corner of Mulligan's bar when this lady called to us from the window of the apartment above the bar. She wanted Anthony to go to the store for her. When we looked up at her, we could see right through her t-shirt to her big, beautiful breasts. We were all staring at her—we did not get many chances to see tits in person.

Anthony said, "What do you want from the store?"

As she was telling Anthony what she wanted, Chubs was saying to me, "Look at those half dollars."

Anthony kept repeating the woman's order to get a longer look at her tits. He kept saying, "Can you tell me what you want again?" Finally, Anthony finished taking the order. He looked at me and Chubs and said, "Titties from heaven. I don't think I can remember what she asked for—I was just thinking about the big, beautiful knockers."

It was just a pleasant surprise that we did not expect. Chubs said, "The best things in life are free."

Chapter Thirteen:

Crazy Friends

It was the summer and I had just finished the seventh grade. A lot of my friends were graduating grammar school so there were parties all over the neighborhood. We were at a graduation party for this girl named Susan, just drinking a few beers and having a pretty mellow time. The kids in the eighth grade were talking about what high school they were going to go to and how they were going to play football. I was only one year away from getting out of grammar school and I was excited for my friends who were going to high school. We were having a pretty relaxing night. It was about 9 PM and I had to be home at 10 PM. The mellow night ended as soon as Stanley showed up at the party. Stanley did not know a mellow time. He had not been there five minutes before he said to us, "Come on, let's go swimming." We asked him where, and he said we'd go to the pool at St. Richard's Apartments. St. Richard's Apartments was an upper class apartment complex; we never thought it was right that they had a pool and we didn't, so at night we would jump the fence and use their pool. It was getting late and I had to go home soon so I did not want to go swimming—plus I hated jumping that big fence.

I told Stanley, "I am not going swimming. I got to go home soon."

He said, "Okay, you stay outside and watch for the cops."

I said okay.

We got up to the pool and there was a security guard sitting in this chair. I told Stanley, "There is a cop sitting by the pool; you can't go in."

He said, "Oh, don't worry, he is just a security guard. If you see the real cops, start yelling and then you run." I stayed outside and my friends jumped the fence. Some of them jumped into the pool and the security guard started yelling at them. Then all of a sudden I saw Stanley—he was running on the side of the pool bare-butt naked toward the security guard. The guard was yelling and Stanley was laughing, naked. I thought, *What the hell is Stanley going to do now?* Stanley ran up to the security guard and pushed him into the pool! Then Stanley jumped in the pool started swimming around the security guard saying, "It feels good, doesn't it?" All of my friends were in the pool laughing and swimming. They did a few laps and then got out and jumped the fence to go home, but Stanley stayed in there with the security guard; it was like they were friends playing in the water. The guard was in the water with his nightstick and hat on. I watched, and Stanley was splashing the guard but they looked like they were having fun. The guard stayed in the pool and swam awhile.

Being with Stanley was more exciting then any action movie you would see in the movies. I think Stanley stayed home and planned these crazy events.

We always went to see a couple of professional baseball games over the summer vacation. We usually went to see the Yankees although my team was the Mets. We would go over to the city about two hours before the game and buy quarts of beer which we drank in the ballpark. We tried to sneak it in, but they were pretty good at catching you. The guy at the gate would say, "Drink it here or leave it here." Most of the time we would just down the beer and go watch the game. We always thought it would not be bad to have the gate job at the ballpark. Look at all the beer this guy can take home.

Stevie was a big baseball fan, and he played pretty good ball, too. He could pitch lefty and righty. If he had had some discipline, he would have been a good ball player. Most of us just did things to have fun and did not learn you needed discipline to make it to the major leagues.

We always got the cheapest seats, which were in the bleachers. If the game got a little boring we would throw Patty out on to the outfield. Usually we threw him out in left field so he did not have to far to run to get to the sidelines; we did not want to interrupt the game too much. Patty never got in trouble because he was so small. He just told the cops, "Listen, these big guys grabbed me and threw me into the outfield." The police would let him go. One time Stevie jumped out on the center field but he hurt his foot and got arrested. He had to go to court and they did not let him back in the ballpark. I guess it was Stevie's way of making it to the big leagues. There is no easy way getting to the big leagues, but Stevie never learned that.

I finally made it to the eighth grade. I felt great and I could not wait until I finished school so I could start working and have some money. I did not know what I was going to do for work but I knew I would get some kind of job and make money. My mother always wanted me to think about going to college but I did not know how to read or write well so I knew I would not last long. While I was in school I was always thinking, *What this teacher is saying was not going to make me money when I got older.*

My mother would talk to my Aunt Rosemary and say, "I don't know what Tony is going to do when he gets older because he is not good in school."

Aunt Rosemary would say, "Well, they always need people to unload trucks."

I would think, *Screw that, Aunt Rosemary, I will join the Mob before I unload trucks.* I thought about driving a truck. I thought about joining the Mob. The guys in the Mob had really nice cars and a lot of money and respect. I knew you had to kill people when you worked for the Mob and I did not want to do that. I thought about owning a bar. There were three bars on my block and all of them were always packed so I figured a bar was a good business. I figured people were always going to drink so I could make money with a bar. My plan was to hire a nice looking blonde with big knockers to be the bartender. She could be nice to the customers but could not screw anybody. I figured half of the bars had guys tending bars so a nice blonde would be sure to draw a crowd. I would have lots of salty food like nuts, chips, and pretzels to keep the customers thirsty. I was confident that my plan would work. Then one day my grandma asked me what I wanted to do when I grew up and I told her I wanted to own a bar. I said, "I think it would be a good business."

She said, "You would make a lot of money, but it is blood money." She said, "Drinking causes a lot of trouble in people's lives and if you own a bar, God is going to punish you. Look at the Kennedy family; they were rich but they got rich off the booze and look at all the bad luck they have had." My grandma always knew things about life that other people did not know. I always listened to her because she was never wrong. After that, I forgot about owning a bar. It was hard to give up the plans with the blonde bartender, but I think my grandma was right.

In the eighth grade, my friends and I were on St. Richard's baseball team. Our baseball coaches' names were Dinger and Bingo. Patty's father would say, "What the hell, Dinger and Bingo, is it a baseball team or a circus?"

We were not real good, but it was nice to be with all of the guys. We practiced or played every day and it gave us something to do. One day I was going to practice and I saw this little kid who had a stick with a string tied to it. He was dangling the string in a puddle. I loved kids so I went over to him and asked him if he had caught anything. He said, "No, but yesterday this guy caught a shark in this pond."

I looked at him and said, "I better not step in that puddle."

He said, "No, there could be another shark in there."

I said, "Good luck with the fishing," and he said goodbye.

We had a Saturday morning game and I got to the ball field early. All of the kids started coming to the baseball field and I started to play catch with Mikey. From a distance I saw Chubs and Chucky. It appeared that they had something on their faces. When they walked closer to me I discovered they had makeup all over them. They had their baseball uniforms on, and they had makeup on. They looked like drag queen baseball players. As soon as I saw them, I was rolling on the ground laughing. I asked them, "What happened to you guys? You look like fruitcakes."

Chubs told me, "Chucky and Stanley slept over my house last night and when Chucky and me woke up we had makeup all over us. Stanley waited until we went to sleep and put makeup all over us. We woke up late and he put so much makeup on us we could not get it all off before we had to leave for the baseball game." Chubs was really upset.

Chucky said, "We are going to get him back." They were both mad but you always knew Stanley was going to do something crazy. There is no way I would have a sleepover and invite Stanley. I thought, *They are lucky that is all that happened to them.*

I saw Stanley in the bleachers. He did not play sports; I think it took too many brain cells for him to think about what he had to do to play. Stanley tried out for football once. When the coach asked him what position he wanted to play he said blocker. I think after the football season he retired from sports. This day, Stanley was in the bleachers laughing, yelling at Chubs saying, "Hey, Chubs, did you have a late date last night?"

I asked Stanley, "What did you do?"

He said, "They look beautiful, don't they." Stanley said, "I told them they better not go to sleep."

Chubs picked up some dirt and rubbed it on his face. He said, "It is better to look dirty than look like a ballerina playing baseball." After awhile Chubs was not mad anymore and we all started laughing. He kept looking at Stanley and saying, "I owe you one, Stanley—you are going to pay for this."

I told Chubs, "Stanley is nuts."

Chubs said, "Yeah, he is nuts. I love him but he is not sleeping over at my house anymore."

Baseball was kind of like school to me. There was too much time when you did not have anything to do so I would start daydreaming. I was not too crazy about baseball but it was fun to be with my friends. Patty got in a run down between first base and second base and he was laughing the whole time they were chasing him. Patty was fast so it took time for them to catch him. He kept laughing and saying, "Ha!" as he ran. I watched another game after ours and this one team was getting their butts kicked. Every player that got on first base was stealing second. I guess their second baseman got a little fed up with the job the catcher was doing. There was a man on first base and on the first pitch, he started to steal second base. The boy stealing second base passed the second baseman, and the second baseman tripped him. Although he was trying to be sneaky about it, the umpire saw him and gave the runner his base. We were all laughing and the second baseman just threw his hands up.

St. Richard's had a basketball team, too. Our coach's name was Chucky. Chucky liked to drink and he came to the games drunk. I don't think we ever practiced. We just played and we always had fun. It was great having Chucky as a coach because if we were on the bench we would just say, "Hey, Chucky, I'm going in now," and he would say okay. One time he was sober and we said, "Chucky, we are going in now," and he said, "Sit down and wait until I call you."

We just said, "Good job, Chucky." I was hoping he was getting off the booze. We never talked bad about the coach because he was nice enough to give us his time to coach us. Every time somebody would start to talk bad about him, we said, "At least he is there for us; nobody else would take the coaching job."

Chucky got replaced by Mr. R., who came in at the middle of the season. He saw we were getting our butts kicked all the time and we got an announcement in school that there would be a basketball meeting after school. We thought, *This is different.*

He gathered us all around and called up the biggest kid, whose name was Edward. Mr. R was a big man, a lot bigger than Edward. Mr. R. took a quarter out of his pocket and said, "Edward, I am going to throw this in the air and whoever gets it, keeps it." He threw the quarter in the air and just stood there as Edward jumped as high as he could and caught the quarter. He let Edward keep the quarter and then he said to us, "Did you see that? I am a lot taller than Edward, a lot stronger than Edward, but he got the quarter because I did not try." He said, "It does not matter who you are or how big you are, it is how hard you try; if you give it all you got, then you will win."

We won a lot of games with Mr. R. as our coach and I never forgot that lesson.

When Muhammad Ali fought George Foreman, Mr. R. bet ten grand on Foreman and lost. He had to leave town for a while. You had to be a responsible gambler in Jersey City or you could wind up dead real quick. I don't think I ever saw Mr. R after that but I kept tabs on him and found out that he got the ten grand together and they did not kill him.

I had great friends in St. Richard's and I knew we would always be friends. I loved my friends but I did not like school. I knew after grammar school I only had four years in high school, then I could get a job.

We finally graduated grammar school. I could not wait to finish school; I was sick of being without money and wanted to work instead of going to school. I think I got lost in about the third grade after my father moved out of the house. I just got lost and the teachers were not good enough to help me catch up with the knowledge I was lacking. After you get lost in school and fall behind, it is so hard to get caught up. Even when I tried to do well in school, I was lost. I know I have to blame myself as much as the teachers, but it was their fault, also. Anyone could teach a smart child, but if a teacher can reach a problem student, he or she is a great teacher.

None of the adults that I knew in Jersey City graduated from college. They all worked hard, and that is all we knew. Most of the adults I knew said school was just something you had to do because if you didn't finish high school, you would not get a good job. A good job to us was a union manual labor job. I wanted to quit school a couple of times but my mother did not let me. She never let me quit anything. If I started a sport and got bored, she said, "You committed to it; you have to go to all the games and practices." She said, "I am not going to let you become a quitter. School is like work; you don't have to like it, but you have to do it."

St. Richard's had a big graduation ceremony for us in the church. As soon as we left the church, all our friends from Thirty-three Schoolyard were waiting for us, lighting fireworks as we walked out of the church. There were bottle rockets going off in the sky and everyone was yelling congratulations. There were parties all over the neighborhood and we started party hopping, going from one house to the other. I drank a little but did not want to get ripped because I knew I would have to see my mother. She was having a party for me, so I went to spend a little time at my house. A lot of my family and friends were there, and my mother had a lot of food and drinks. I did not want to bring a lot of my friends to my house because there were a lot of kids that were drunk. As soon as I got in the house, my family and friends congratulated me. Aunt Rosemary said, "Have you been drinking? Let me smell your breath."

I thought, *Oh, no, I am going to get busted,* but I gave her a kiss and she stopped busting my chops.

You had to take a test to get into Catholic high school. I was a dumb in school but I had street smarts. My neighbor Steven W. had gotten in trouble at school and had to stay after and work to make up for it. They made him throw some boxes away, but when he opened them, he saw they were full of high school entrance exams. I paid Steven two bucks for a test. Steven told me, "If you tell anybody I am going to kick your butt." You learned how to keep your mouth shut in Jersey City.

My friend Tony and I studied hard for the high school test. I was one of the worst students in the class but I got one of the highest grades. The nun that was my teacher said to me, "Tony, you really surprised me. You really did great on that test." All I could think is, *Thank God, you made my neighbor Steven stay after school that day.* The test was not the same as the year before, but it was close enough so that I knew what they were asking. I got accepted into all the schools I applied to.

Chapter Fourteen:

High School

I went to St. Ike's High School, but most of my friends went to St. Paul's Catholic High School or Jersey City Public High School. I thought it would be good to go to school with different people. Maybe I could learn something. I only knew Tony B., who was a friend of mine, but we were not in any classes together. Most of the kids were normal at St. Ike's, not as crazy as the kids from St. Richard's. Everything was pretty normal until science class, when I meet this kid named Al. Al was like me, not big on the school thing. We both were lost in the first science class. I was hoping Al could help me, but no luck—he was just as brilliant as me. The teacher gave us a break from class to go get a drink of water or to use the bathroom. Al and I stayed in the classroom to talk while the other kids went outside. He said, "Watch what I am going to do."

He wrote a note to this a kid that looked smart, but he was a little goofy.

Al got finished writing and handed me the note. It said, "Hi, my name is Maria and I am madly in love with you. I will wait for you after school at the pizza place. I can't wait to see you. Love, Maria." I was just thinking Al was St. Richard's material. Al ran over and put the note under the smart kid's book while he was still out on break. When class started again, the kid found the note and kept looking at this nice-looking girl, Maria. At first I felt sorry for him but then I said to myself, *Well, at least he is having a nice thought right now.* Al and I were laughing the whole class. I did not learn anything in science class. Al was always making me laugh. What Al had to say was more interesting than what the teacher was saying. One time we had to cut these frogs up and look inside the body to identify its body parts. This kid Mahoney said, "Let's see if this teacher is smart. I bet he does not know everything about these frogs." Mahoney was chewing gum and he put a piece of gum in the frog's stomach. He called the teacher over and asked what was in the frog's stomach. The teacher said some scientific term, and Mahoney said, "You are full of it, that is a piece of gum." The teacher got embarrassed because we knew he tried to lie to us. One thing about kids is, if you lie to them and you get caught, you lose respect. Whenever the teacher called on Mahoney to ask him questions, Mahoney always stood up and shook his hand and said, "The basic fundamentals of this problem is I don't have a clue and that is what you should have said about the gum in the frog's stomach." The teacher had lost control of the science class and it became a big joke. The teacher had the last laugh, though; he failed half the class and they had to go to summer school. I liked my summers too much and if I knew I might have to go to summer school, I studied my butt off. I got a D in science—not a great grade, but I passed. My mother gave me a hard time about the D grade but when I told her half of the class failed, she put things into perspective. I think we got the teacher fired, or he did not want to put up with smart-butt kids anymore, because that was his first and last year teaching at our school.

One year I was failing two classes, English and math, and I thought I would have to go to summer school. I had a meeting with my career counselor, a nun. She told me that if I stayed after school and came in early before school started she could help me. That nun taught me more in one day than the other teachers taught me all year. I got Bs on the final exam in both classes, and I did not have to go to summer school, all because that nun helped me.

I always got along with the kids at high school but I still hung out with my friends from Thirty-three Schoolyard. I went to school football games and school dances with the kids from St. Ike's and all the kids were cool. I never had any trouble being from a different neighborhood until one day when I was sitting in class and three of the girls in the class were crying. I did not know what was going on with the girls, but I knew it was something bad.

One of the girls had to leave the class because she was crying so much. I was trying to figure out what was going on This kid in class I was cool with asked me if I was a friend with Blinky, one of the kids from Thirty-three Schoolyard. I said yes and he told me to tell him the next time he saw my friend driving in a car he was going to throw a brick through the window. I still did not know what was going on. When the teacher asked one of the girls what had happened, they said that one of their girlfriends had been killed the night before when the car they were in hit a telephone pole. The guys that were driving told the police that my friends had thrown a brick through the car window and made them crash. I did not know what to do, I felt so bad because the girls had lost their friend. I could not talk bad about my friends because I was taught that whatever your friends did, you did not talk bad about them in front of other people. I was taught that you brought it up to them face to face. There was nothing I could do to help these girls. I felt so bad that my stomach was hurting. I told the kid was not a good idea to throw bricks. All of the kids in class felt bad. I could not wait to get out of school and back to my friends to see what happened. All of my friends were hanging out and drinking in the cellar of the kid called Rat. Anthony called everybody together and said, "You know what people are saying, that we did something bad." He said, "And nobody has said anything to our faces, but we know you guys have been talking about it." He said, "It is all bull crap and you know I don't lie to my friends." That is all I had to hear. I trusted Anthony and I knew he was telling the truth. I almost got into a couple of fights because the kids at St. Ike's blamed my friends for killing that girl. I just held my ground and I did not fight with anybody because I knew a lot of people were hurt over what happened. My friends had to go to court and everybody found out that they did not throw the brick through the window. The driver was high on drinking and drugs and he hit the pole without any help from my friends. Instead of taking it like a man, he tried to have my friends take the fall for what he did. A few years later, the same three guys were driving and getting high again and they crashed. One of the guys got his legs caught under the motor of the car and the other two guys ran away from the accident. He was paralyzed for the rest of his life. After the kids from St. Ike's found out that my friends did not throw the brick, they were cool with me again. Sometimes you have to ride out the tough times. I always had faith in my friends and would be glad to take a beating for any of them.

This kid, Frank S., came to St. Ike's from public school. I knew of a kid getting thrown out of public school and put into Catholic school before, but Frank had taken so many hits of acid his parents had him put in Catholic School to get him away from the drugs. Frank was nuts. He told me if he ran down the block as fast as he could he would get an acid flashback. I never believed in the flashbacks before I meet Frank. Frank would get up in the middle of class and just start walking around the classroom. I guess all the teachers knew his story because they never yelled at him when he would get up and walk around and say, "Wow, it is beautiful." I liked to hang out with Frank because he was always laughing. He did not drink or do drugs anymore but I think he still had enough drugs in his system to keep him high for a lifetime. I sat in the lunch room with Frank and he said, "All right, I am bored, let's make believe everyone one in here is nude. Okay, now, you really have to picture them naked." If a fat girl passed by us, he would be on the floor laughing. I laughed with him so hard I would get a headache. Frank always joked unless he was playing sports. He was very good in basketball and baseball and when I went to see him play it was like watching another person, he was so serious. Just seeing Frank go into his flashbacks was enough to make me hate acid. We did not have many drugs in our school, but during the seventies, pot was everywhere.

Al and Tony B. got busted smoking pot in this park by school. Al's father did not speak English, just Spanish. The principal called Tony's mother and Al's father to the school and was telling them that the kids had gotten caught smoking pot. If they got caught again, they would be expelled from school. In the middle of the principal's speech, Al said, "Hold on, I have to tell my father what you are saying because he does not speak English." Al turned to his father and told him, "He called you in here today because he wanted you and Tony's mother to know that we are the best students he has in his school." Al's father looked at the principal and smiled and said, "Gracias."

Most teachers did not scare me but we had one English teacher that was from Ireland and she was a little nuts. If you did not do your homework she would go nuts. English was the only class I did my homework in, and I did it every day because I did not want this teacher going off on me. I got an A in her class because I knew I had better do my homework. If all the teachers were like her, I would have been an A student. The English teacher scared me, but she did not scare Al. One day she was yelling at us, and in the middle of her yelling, Al started yelling, "Oh, no, not here, I think I am going to, I think I am going to." Then he made a sounds like he was cumming and he was shaking his body. The English teacher was a little nuts, but Al was nuttier then her. She kicked Al out of the classroom, but the whole class laughed non-stop for at least fifteen minutes. I was laughing so hard I was crying. I do not think the teacher knew what to do after that episode. She just sat in her chair and said, "Okay, calm down."

We had a disciplinarian at St. Ike's who called you into his office if you got into trouble. One day I was walking down the hall and saw that somebody had taped a picture of this nude woman to the door of the disciplinarian's office. The woman had big boobs and had her legs spread wide open. Everyone in the hall was laughing as they went by the picture. All I could think of is, *The person that did this is nuts!* Everyone was laughing, but they were passing the disciplinarian's office fast because they did not want to be in front of the door when he came out to see why everyone was laughing. I usually stayed out of trouble at St. Ike's because I was not with my friends from Thirty-three Schoolyard so everything was kind of mellow.

But one day, we had to go on a religious retreat instead of going to school.

The retreat was in this office building away from school. I always liked to learn about God and religion, but this retreat was goofy. Most of the time they were not talking about God; it was like a feel-good class. My friend Anthony P. said to me, "Let's get out of here."

It was Friday, so when they released us for lunch, Anthony and I took off and went to drink beer. I had a good weekend and was not thinking about the fact that I cut out of the religious retreat, but when I got to homeroom on Monday morning, there were notes for Anthony and me to go and see the disciplinarian. Anthony and I went into his office and sat outside in a waiting room until he called us in. Most of the time it was not the punishment that bothered me, it was the waiting. Anthony said, "Let me go in his office first. This has to be about us leaving early from the retreat." He did not say anything else; we just waited there silently. The disciplinarian opened the door and Anthony went in. The disciplinarian left the door open so I could hear and see Anthony talking when the disciplinarian asked him why he did not return to the religious retreat on Friday. Anthony said he had had diarrhea and he had crapped his pants. He said, "I had to go home. I had a bad stomach pain and I could not return." I was outside the office laughing. I did not expect Anthony to come up with a story like that.

The disciplinarian did not know what to do so he said, "Okay, Anthony I hope your feel better."

Usually I thought of what to say pretty fast but I was just thinking about Anthony saying he crapped himself and I could not think. The disciplinarian called me in to the office and asked me why I had left early. I told him the truth. I said, "Listen, the thing was boring and stupid, I was not learning anything, and I left." He gave me a week's detention. I knew better than to tell the truth, but I could not beat the crap-in-the-pants story and I did not want to use the same one. That is the first and last time I had to go to detention.

At least they cared enough to check to make sure we went to class. In public school there were so many kids they did not even keep track of who was there. If the kids cut classes, most of the teachers did not report them. Most of my friends that went to public high school never graduated.

I was always happy to hear the last bell in school; that meant the fun time was about to begin. One afternoon school was over and I was getting my books out of my locker to go home when two girls I hung out with in Thirty-three Schoolyard came up to me with a newspaper article; there was a picture of a car driven through a Laundromat window. They said, "Look at this picture in the newspaper." I looked at it and read the article. This girl, Karen, whom I knew from St. Richard's, had driven a car through a Laundromat window. I asked Susan what had happened and she said, "Kathy took Karen to her driving test. Karen passed the test and asked Kathy if she could drive home. She was doing good driving and then she just hung a right turn, smack into the Laundromat window."

I was on the floor laughing. The paper had a picture of the car sitting on top of the washing machines. Thank God, nobody got hurt. About a year later, Karen was teaching me how to drive down by Roosevelt Stadium. She was showing me how to back up and she almost hit this woman driving a car. Later I was driving and I almost hit the same woman. I could hear the woman say, "Crap, I have to get out of here before they kill me."

Chapter Fifteen:

Don't Play with Fireworks

It was a hot summer day right after the Fourth of July. Some of my friends had started driving and had cars so a bunch of us were going to go down the Jersey Shore to go fishing. Jake had a car and Anthony had a car. We all met down at Thirty-three Schoolyard and got all the fishing poles in the car. I got in Jake's car but we wanted to by some beer first, so we started driving to a bar and one of the guys from the other car was shooting leftover bottle rockets at us. We just closed the car window. When we got to the bar, we all got out of the car and they shot another bottle rocket at us and it hit the curb and went up into the air. We all went in the bar and bought two cases of beer. When we got outside, we could see fire coming out of a house in back of the bar. We saw that the bottle rocket had broken the window and started a fire. We all had to think fast; Sonny said, "Somebody pull the fire alarm." Anthony M. ran to so that, and Sonny said, "We can't leave because there might be some kids in the house." He ran up to the house and rang the doorbell but nobody was home. We could not do anything more to help the house so when we heard the fire trucks coming we all piled into the cars and took off. We knew if we stayed there, we would have gotten arrested and our parents would have gotten stuck with the bills for repairing the house. Jake was hauling butt down the highway when we heard a loud noise. His muffler had fallen off on the highway. We stopped the car and the muffler was hot so hot that we put some ice cubes on it, threw it in the car, and took off. Jake kept saying, "Look in the back to see if any cops are coming after us." I was looking out of the back window and there were no police in sight. We got out of Jersey

City fast. We did not talk much about the house; we all felt bad about it but there was nothing we could do. We started talking about fishing.

We stopped in this small town before we got to the ocean and went into the local supermarket to look for some bait. Anthony asked the butcher for some scraps of meat for fishing bait and he gave us two big garbage bags full of red meat. We got to Sandy Hook and started fishing. We were all drinking and fishing and having a good time, but nobody caught any fish so we went skinny-dipping. We got done skinny-dipping and it was late so we got all the poles in the car. Chubs said, "What are we going to do with all this meat?"

Jake said, "Throw it in the water; the fish will eat it."

We got back in Jersey City about 12 AM and everything was calm. We stayed away from the schoolyard that night. We did not talk about the fire. We all knew that we had to keep our mouths shut about what happened. We all met down Thirty-three Schoolyard early the next morning. Sonny had the newspaper and he was reading about the fire. We all thanked God that no one was hurt in the fire. I said, "Sonny, did any kids live there?"

He said, "It does not say it the paper."

I said, "I hope they did not lose anything."

He said, "No, the paper said the firefighters put out the fire right away."

We also found out the there was a shark attack in Sandy Hook. Nobody got hurt but there were sharks all over the shoreline. We all said, "Crap, we could not catch anything and now there are sharks all over the place."

Sonny said, "I hope those people got insurance to pay for all of the damage from the fire." That was the last time we shot bottle rockets at each other. We still shot them up in the air but we would not shoot them at each other. Most of us learned a lesson from this experience.

Tex, however, usually did not learn from the lessons of life. One night I went down to the schoolyard and Tex was down there sitting on the stairs. He did not look too good so I asked him what was wrong. He said, "I shot a bottle rocket at a cop and hit him in the head."

"That is about the dumbest thing I ever heard in my life. Tex, what were you thinking about?"

"Crap, that cop was fast—he almost caught me."

"Sure. You pissed him off. You run a lot faster when you are pissed off."

"You are right."

I said, "Tex, that is not the smartest thing to do. Shooting a bottle rocket at a cop is about the dumbest thing I ever heard of."

"I guess you are right," he said. "I just thought it would be funny. But once that cop got close to me I thought he was going to kick my butt. I had to turn on the speed or he would have got me."

I told him, "You are lucky he did not shoot you." You did not want to piss cops off—they could make your life very tough. I always worried about Tex; he did not mind being arrested.

All the cops knew Tex's address by heart. If the cops asked him his name, they would nod when he answered and say, "Yes, you live at—" and they would say his address. Tex had some older brothers that kept the police in business. My father always told me, "Do not piss off the cops because if they got a crime they cannot solve and you pissed them off, they can pin the crime on you."

I liked the cops in Jersey City—they were nice to me for the most part and they gave us a lot of breaks. Most of them grew up in Jersey City and they had done the same crap we did when they were kids. They were just doing their jobs; they had to feed their families. If you gave the cops respect, they treated you good. If you disrespected the cops, they gave you a hard time right back.

Chapter Sixteen:

Boxing

I started boxing at the age of sixteen. I got my butt kicked a lot in Jersey City so I was pretty tough but I did not know how to fight. I always wanted to learn how to fight because I figured in Jersey City, fighting well was a priority. I looked into taking karate but the class was thirty dollars a month and I did not have that money. My friend Patty said, "Let's go to Left's Gym; it is only seven dollars a month."

I said I could afford seven dollars a month, so we went.

The people in Jersey City loved fighting. If you watched a baseball game on TV and they had a fight, all people would be talking about was the fight. A lot of people only watched hockey for the fights. Boxing cut right to the chase: two guys putting on the gloves to beat the crap out of each other. We loved action, and boxing was full of action. I loved boxing because it was not boring like other sports; there was action every second.

I will never forget the first time I went to Left's Gym. It was a rainy spring day. Left's Gym looked like a house from the outside but there was a little wooden sign on the top of the front door that said Left's Gym on it, with two boxing gloves. As soon as you walked into the gym, you could smell the sweat. When you walked in the front door, you entered a dark hallway and you had to walk up the stairs to get to the gym. There were a couple of old pool tables in the front room and then you walked into a door that was a small dressing room. The room past the dressing room was the gym. The boxing gym consisted of a boxing ring, two heavy bags, and speed bag. I paid the seven bucks to Lefty. He was a short man who had a few teeth missing. He owned the gym and trained many of the fighters. Lefty had been around the fight game most of his life, and he did not trust many people. You had to earn his respect before he liked you. When I first started boxing, I did not have a good diet and I smoked cigarettes and drank beer. The cigarettes really hurt my boxing because I could do well the first two rounds but by the third round I was out of air and usually got my butt kicked. I knew I had to quit smoking to become a good boxer.

The first boxer I saw in Left's Gym was Hollywood. He was a huge dude that looked like you could hit him with a sledgehammer and he would just smile at you before he killed you. I had heard of Hollywood but I had never seen him before. I was scared just looking at him. Hollywood was the toughest guy I ever met in my life. Hollywood boxed and owned a bar. He made a living fighting. He was not the best boxer in the world but he was tough and he learned how to make money out of the sport. Hollywood was the professional state champ of New Jersey. To some people that did not mean a whole lot, but to me, he was the toughest of the many tough guys in New Jersey. He had a lot of girlfriends and he drove a big Cadillac with license plates that said Hollywood. He had it made: the bar, a lot of girls, and a nice car.

Hollywood fought a lot of world champions and whoever else would fight him for money. One time they were having a wrestling-against-boxing match over in New York City. Hollywood was scheduled to fight a wrestler. We asked him, "Are you really going to fight that huge wrestler?"

Hollywood said, "I would fight a tiger for twenty-five grand."

He was always nice to me. One day Patty and I were sitting in the gym after we finished working out and Hollywood walked in. Lefty said, "Hey, Hollywood, tell the kids the story about when you fought for the championship of the world."

Hollywood said, "The champ was beating me up pretty good and I sat down on the stool after the round was over. The referee came over to me and asked me if I was doing okay. I said, 'Yes, I'm fine.' The referee put up some fingers and asked me, 'How many fingers do I have up?'" Hollywood said, "How many guesses do I get?"

Hollywood sparred with this big guy named Cowboy. They beat the crap out of each other every day and I sat and watched them every time they sparred. Neither one of them listened to the boxing coaches; they were just tough guys. Hollywood would hold you and hit you. Hollywood and Cowboy clinched a lot and Lefty said, "Are you boxing or making love?" To Hollywood and Cowboy, boxing was more like street fighting. This is how they made their living so they did whatever they had to do to get paid. I saw Hollywood fight in boxing matches on TV and the only reason he lost was that the fight was stopped on cuts. I never saw him get hurt. He would just start bleeding and they would stop the fight.

Cowboy was a real character. He jumped rope like a little girl. Most boxers skipped rope with a leather rope, but Cowboy would jump rope slowly with a clothing line jump rope like the ones the girls used on the street. I think he loved to fight but did not like any of the other exercises boxers had to do. When he hit the heavy bag, it would go flying from side to side. Cowboy wore a big cowboy hat and had no front teeth. One time he was training for a fight and this newspaper reporter came to the gym to interview him. Cowboy was jumping rope and the reporter started asking him questions about the fight and his opponent. Cowboy replied, "He is a tough fighter but I am the more experienced fighter and I will beat him."

The reporter asked Cowboy if he drank alcohol. Cowboy said, "No, I can't drink because I am an alcoholic."

"Do you smoke cigarettes?"

"Nope."

The reporter was thinking and I think he ran out of questions. Cowboy, still jumping rope, must have felt bad that the reporter ran out of questions so he said, "But I smoke pot." Everyone in the gym was cracking up, Cowboy still jumping rope with a big smile on his face, not afraid to reveal his two missing front teeth. Everybody stopped what they were doing in the gym and just started laughing. We must have laughed for ten minutes and then Lefty said, "Okay, guys, get back to work."

Cowboy lost that fight. I did not see it but I asked Lefty what happened. Lefty said, "Cowboy ate a piece of the pie." I did not know what that meant so after I got done working out I asked another boxer. He said, "It means you get laid the night before the fight and you have weak legs."

I really loved being at the gym with these tough guys. They were really humble and did not have to act tough because they were tough. One time this kid that was new to boxing was jumping rope. He was tripping over the rope a lot and one of the boxers was laughing at him. Cowboy walked up to the guy that was laughing and said, "Hey, we don't laugh at people here; we are all learning. If you don't try, you don't learn."

It was great being at Left's with all of these tough guys. I met a lot of people that fought world champions and a lot of boxers that fought on TV. They were all nice to me. It did not matter if they won or lost, it was the guts they had to get in the ring and give it their best. Any time I watched them fight I felt like I was in there fighting with them. Once in awhile they would pull off a win and I felt great for them.

Donnie taught me how to punch by hitting the heavy bag. The first day I was at the gym, Donnie said to me, "Okay, let's see your boxing stance." I held my two hand high by my shoulders and he looked at me and said, "We are going to have to work on that fighting stance of yours a little bit." He showed me where to keep my feet and where to keep my hands. He taught me how to move so I was on balance to throw punches. Donnie had the patience of a saint. He was one of the best teachers I ever had in my life, and he never said anything negative. He sat on a stool next to the heavy bag and he'd say, "Okay, try this." He'd get off of his stool and show you how to throw the punches. Donnie taught me how to throw the punches straight in so the opponent could not see them coming. He gave you numbers and each number meant a different combination. After my first lesson, he told me that I was doing so good that he was going to give me an extra number to practice. That really built up my confidence because I knew I was not doing too great, but he told me I was, so it made me feel good. As time passed, I watched Donnie with the new guys and he told all of them the same thing: "You are doing good so I am going to give you an extra number."

Donnie taught you how to throw punches, but there is a whole lot more too boxing than that. I did not know it at the time, but if you listened to this little, sweet man and punched the way he told you to punch, you would really hurt your opponent. The problem was that most people do not listen; they think they know everything. I listened to everything Donnie taught me.

When I first started working out, all I did was hit the bag and jump rope. Lefty came over to me one day and said, "Boxing is like dancing. Until you dance, you are not going to learn how to fight." Lefty said, "You have to get in the ring and spar so you can learn how to box."

The first time I sparred, I fought a black kid that beat the crap out of me. He was fast and used my head as a speed bag. After I was done, Lefty looked at me and said, "You did well." He told me the kid was good and I did not give up. Lefty wanted to see if I would take a beating and come back. I did not know how to box yet but I knew how to take a beating. Lefty and his brother Donnie always encouraged me.

At my next sparring match, I decided that I was not going to let the guy use my head as a speed bag. I still did not know how to box but I was going to do all I could to hold my ground. Once the bell sounded, I picked up the kid, threw him in the corner, and kept punching him. I did not stop punching; I figured I would not give the kid a chance to hit me. Every time he tried to get off the ropes I picked him up and threw him back and kept punching. After the sparring match was over, the kid told me he would never spar with me again because I was crazy. I thought crazy was a good thing in the boxing world.

Patty had his first boxing match in a Catholic high school in Jersey City. Patty and I walked to the school about 7 PM. When we got to the school gym it was packed. This boxer named Pat O. from Duncan Avenue was going to fight a guy named Twisted, who was from Greenville. Both kids came from tough neighborhoods and their neighborhoods were there to support them. A gang named the Shamrocks from Greenville was at the fight and the boys from Duncan Ave. were there. There were motorcycles gangs and thugs from different parts of Jersey City. I knew that the fight in the crowd was going to be bigger than the fight in the ring. You learn at a young age that there is going to be trouble and you have to plan on where to locate yourself to have a better chance of staying unharmed and out of the trouble. I sat near the ringside. I figured the gangs were up in the bleachers and the fights would break out there. I had an exit door picked out in case someone started shooting a gun.

Patty was nervous and kept talking. I had a lot of respect for Patty; he had balls for getting in the ring to fight. We had not been boxing for too long and Lefty told me I was not ready to fight in a real boxing match yet. Patty was a good boxer. I sparred with him and Lefty used to call us the Heavyweight and the Paperweight because I was fat and Patty was skinny.

They were selling beer at the fight and even the guy that was going to sing the National Anthem was having a few beers. Everyone was hanging out and I knew there was going to be a few fights in the crowd—I could feel it in the air. The man that was drinking beer got inside the ring to sing the National Anthem. He said, "Can you please stand for the singing of the National Anthem?" and everyone got on their feet. We were all excited to get the fights started. He got halfway through the National Anthem and said, "This is too hard." He got out of the ring and returned to his beer. Everyone in the gym was laughing and we finished singing the National Anthem for him.

The announcer came into the ring to announce the first boxing match. Patty was fighting this kid from Greenville in the first bout of the night. I was glad because I wanted his fight to be over. He was too nervous. Hollywood was the guest referee. I could see Donnie twiddling his thumbs when Patty was getting ready to box. Patty was doing good—he was moving, blocking punches, and jabbing the kid with his left hand. He kept smashing his jab into the kid's face. I knew Patty would hurt the kid if he hit him with a left hook; he had a good left hook, and I knew it because he had hit me with it a few times. I kept yelling at Patty to throw his left hook.

I guess Patty was getting pissed at me because he was so nervous. He finally looked at me and said, "Shut up." As soon as he looked at me, the kid hit him with a punch. I started laughing. It was the only punch the kid hit him with the whole fight. Patty clearly won the fight but the judges called it a draw. Hollywood told us the next day that the judge didn't want to hurt the boxers' feelings because Patty and the other kid were so young. Patty received a boxing trophy and was happy that he did well in his first boxing match. I was really proud of him for doing so good in a real boxing match. He got dressed and came out to sit with me. I hugged him and said, "Patty, you did great."

He smiled and said thanks.

The main event featured another boxer from Greenville against the boxer from Duncan Avenue. Both of them were in high school. This was the fight that most people came to see. As soon as the boxers started making their way to the ring, fights broke out between the two neighborhoods. There were so many fights in the stands you could not even pay attention to the boxing match. I knew some of these kids carried guns so I was thinking more about the fights in the crowd than the fight in the ring. People were throwing things in the air. It got so out of hand that the police came in to put a stop to the fights in the stands. Twisted, the kid from Greenville, won the fight. He would go away to jail a couple of years later for stabbing a kid to death.

I never saw a boxing crowd like the boxing crowd in Jersey City. I guess we were taught that if your friend is getting beat up, you have to jump in and help him. The fans could not stand their friends getting beat up, so they wanted to be part of the action. You could see people in the stands moving and throwing punches like they were fighting. The fans cheered their favorite boxers. I was excited about being able to fight in front of a big crowd. For me there was nothing more exciting in the world more than boxing in front of a Jersey City crowd.

I was learning how to punch well but I needed a lot of work on my defense. At first, I was taking many punches because I did not know how to block them. Patty knew how to block punches really well, so I asked him to teach me how. One Saturday morning we went down Thirty-three Schoolyard with the boxing gloves and Patty showed me how to block the punches. We were the only ones in the schoolyard at that time. He started throwing punches at me; he would punch me in the face and laugh and say, "Pat it away. It is like playing patty cake, you just pat it away." After he punched me in the face about fifteen times, I started getting the hang of it and started blocking punches. Patty said, "Yeah, you got it now." We both started laughing. After that lesson I knew how to block punches, which was an advantage because a lot of boxers did not do a good job at blocking. They just concentrated on punching. I knew I was not going to make it as a boxer if I did not know how to block punches. I would get headaches after I sparred from taking so many punches to the head. I would dance like Ali but when they cornered me, I had to punch or be punched. Equipped with my new skill, I was ready to do a good job fighting.

I started to spar with the pros in Left's Gym. I sparred with Hollywood a few times, and he took it easy on me. I danced my butt off not to let him get close to me. He hit me with three punches and cut me over the eye. He only hit me with three shots but it was enough to wobble my legs. He came over to me after we sparred and said, "I did not want to hurt you but it is a tough game and you have to be tough in the fight game."

I said, "That is okay, Hollywood, thanks for not killing me."

It was cool being sixteen and being able to say I sparred with Hollywood. Patty, Jake, and I started working out hard because we wanted to fight in the New Jersey Golden Gloves. I lost about twenty-five pounds to fight in the light heavy weight class. Jake was a light heavy weight, too, so we sparred with each other. When we first started to spar we would start laughing but we would beat each other up pretty good. Lefty called us the Gladiators because we went at it every time we sparred. I learned a lot sparring with Jake; it seemed like whoever got mad first would lose the sparring match. You could not get mad. You had to think about what you were doing. You could have a controlled anger but you couldn't get mad. I loved Jake and we knew beating the crap out of each other was just going to make us better fighters.

Fighting in Left's was like fighting in a real fight. If you could not take a beating, you did not belong in Left's. When you sparred with the pros, they would work with you hard. If you were younger, they would not try to kill you, but it only took one punch by them and they would put a hurting on you. One time they brought this kid up to Left's to spar with one of the pros. The kid was from a different gym but he was supposed to be a Golden Glove champ. Johnny S. was a nice, quiet guy; he was not that fast with his hands, but he had a great right cross. This kid was going off on Johnny. The kid was really pounding him with good shots. I finished working out and was just sitting by the ring watching the sparring match. I kept thinking I hope this kid has a good chin because he is going to make Johnny mad and if Johnny connects with a right hand, he is going to hurt the kid.

Sure enough, Johnny took two rounds of the kid throwing a lot of punches at him, and Johnny threw one right hand that landed on the kid's jaw and sent him flying to the canvas. The kid hit the ring hard and everyone stopped for a second but then they continued to work out. The kid's legs were wobbling and Johnny said, "Are you okay?"

I saw Johnny knock this guy out on the Wide World of Sports on TV with one punch, also. Johnny took a beating for about eight rounds and then threw one punch that connected right on the guy's chin. That guy did not get up until after the count of ten. After this kid left the gym, Lefty said, "You got to respect the pros; don't throw down unless you want to go down." I learned an important lesson that day—only put out what you can take. If a guy was working with you, you should just move around and work on your jab but you always had to be able to protect yourself because most pros in Left's knew how to punch hard.

Boxing matches were always a lot of excitement. You never knew what you were going to see. I don't think I ever went to see a boxing match when there were not fights in the crowd. Lefty would always say, "If they are so tough, why don't they just get in the ring and fight?" Lefty was always ready to sign up a new fighter. Patty, Jo, and I would go to see a professional boxer from Left's fight once or twice a month.

One time this fighter looked very good in the ring but he did not throw any punches. He just danced around and he was not hit a lot but he lost the fight because he did not punch. He went to the locker room and changed his clothes and then went to sit next to his wife. The boxer looked real sharp in a suit with a black hat on. As soon as he sat down, his wife started beating him up. She said, "I told you if you did not throw punches, I was going to kick your butt." She knocked him right off his chair.

Another night two boxers were fighting and this big guy was walking up and down the aisle rooting for one of them. This guy looked like a pimp, with a cane, a big fur coat, and a fur hat. After the second round I was getting tired of listening to this guy. The second round ended and the guy looked at these three little Italian guys and said, "I can do the same thing to you." As soon as he said that, with a flash one of the little Italian guys stood up and punched him in the jaw. The big guy was laid out on his back. The little Italian guy just sat back down calmly. Everyone in the crowd was cheering for the little guy. The big guy did not open his mouth the rest of the night. That was what was great about Jersey City in those day—you got your butt kicked if you deserved it and the cops never got involved.

The best fight I ever saw was between Rock and this guy Johnny from Bayonne that trained in Left's Gym. Rock had just gotten out of prison. *Sports Illus-*

trated did an article on him. In the article, Rock said boxing was nothing to him because in prison he would fight with three guards that had clubs. He said fighting one guy without a weapon was a piece of cake. Patty and I went to see the fight; we had seen this guy in *Sports Illustrated Magazine* and were excited to see him in person. He looked tough in the magazine. The fight was in a bingo hall in West New York, New Jersey. Patty and I could get into the locker rooms because we knew all the boxers.

Rock looked scary. He was not a big man but every inch of his body was solid muscle. Rock looked liked he had muscles on his head. Patty went over to him and said, "Yeah, Rock, good luck tonight in your fight."

Rock said, "Thanks a lot, kid," and shook Patty's hand.

Patty looked at me and said, "He looks scary. That Rock looks like Frankenstein."

Watching Rock fight was not like watching a boxing match. Watching Rock fight was more like watching a death match. Whoever got in the ring with Rock was lucky to get out alive. We all thought that Johnny from Left's was going to get killed. We were all cheering for Johnny but we were also hoping Rock did well because of the tough life he had. Patty said, "That Johnny's got some huge balls on him. I would not get in the ring with Rock."

When I looked at Rock I thought, *How the hell do you hurt this guy, he has muscles everywhere?*

As soon as the bell rang, they started beating the crap out of each other. I have never seen a fight like this before—it was nonstop action. Johnny was holding his ground; as hard as he was getting hit, he stayed in there and hit Rock with some hard shots. He traded hard blows with Rock. The fight was going back and forth. There was no defense at all involved in this fight. It was two tough guys laying it all on the line. Rock was hitting Johnny so hard that his hairpiece came loose. Nobody knew that Johnny wore a hairpiece until that night. Every time Rock snapped his head back with a punch, Johnny's hair flew off the top of his head. All eyes were focused on the fight—we did want to miss a second of action. I knew the fight would end in a knockout because both fighters where trading powerful punches. Even Patty, who loved cracking jokes, did not say much about the wig. Even though it was one of the funniest things we ever saw in our lives, our eyes were concentrated on the punches. Between the rounds all we could say was, "Wow." The fans were going crazy cheering for Rock or Johnny. I guess Johnny had some Superglue on the back of his head that held that hairpiece on, because every time he got punched, the hairpiece would snap back but it would fall back into the perfect place.

I never saw two guys take so many hard punches in my life. Both fighters began to bleed from cuts over their eyes. What a fight. The cheering crowd stayed on its feet for most of the fight. After six rounds of hard punches, both fighters were cut badly. The doctor looked at Rock and said he could not continue. They should have called in a draw because both of the boxers were bleeding badly, but Johnny had home court advantage, and in boxing, that means a lot. Johnny won the fight. He deserved his night of glory because he earned it; he stayed in there and traded with one of the toughest men in the world. Johnny came out of the ring and the fans carried him back to the dressing room. Patty went over as Rock was getting out of the ring and said, "Good fight, Rock, you will win next time you fight."

Rock said, "They should not have stopped the fight but that is how it goes sometimes."

Patty said, "Great fight."

Rock did not look too mad; he knew he did his best and the doctor stopped the fight. The decision was out of his hands.

I don't know how much the two fighters got paid for that fight, but I know they did not get paid enough. A few months after that fight, they had a rematch in New York and Johnny got knocked out cold in the third round. I had a lot of respect for Johnny; that was his only great fight, but it was the greatest fight I ever saw in my life.

Rock started to do good for himself. He was fighting and making commercials and it seemed like he was always on TV. Rock had a problem with some people in New York and they shot him with a shotgun in a clothing store. I think they shot him six times and left him for dead. The gunshots did not kill Rock; I guess all of those muscles protected him, but the shotgun blew off some of his fingers. He still wanted to box. Rock found out who shot him and burnt his house down, and he was sent back to prison. I was really sad that he had to go back to prison even though I did not know him. I was hoping he would become successful. Rock only knew two things: boxing and jail. I don't think Rock chose his life; stuff happens when you are born in a tough neighborhood. In a tough neighborhood, burning somebody's house down after they try to kill you is the right thing to do.

I started to spar with Lucky, the New Jersey Light Heavyweight champion. He was a good-looking Irish kid about twenty years old and he was a great boxer. Lucky's head was shaved; he had tattoos on his arms, wore a diamond ring, and had a gold earring in his ear. Lucky was from Greenville, a section of Jersey City, and he hung out with a gang called the Shamrocks. Every time Lucky fought, there would be hundreds of Shamrocks in the audience. It was always a big event because they drove motorcycles and they were all nuts. Lucky was a knockout artist. I watched him hit the heavy bag in the gym. When he hit it with his right hand, he pivoted with his right foot and hit the bag with all of his weight. Lucky broke the bag a few times.

When Lucky boxed and started to connect with the right hand, it was only a matter of time before he knocked out his opponent. When we sparred, he'd hit me in the middle of the nose and give me two black eyes. He must have been aiming there because he did not want to knock me out. I still remember the first time he hit me with a right hand. I heard Lefty said, "The kid took my right hand and that is a good thing."

I think my teachers in school thought I was an abused kid because I always had black eyes. When they asked me what happened, I told them, "I am a boxer."

One time I was hanging out on the corner with my friends and Lucky was selling his boxing tickets in Mulligan's bar. When he came out of Mulligan's, he spotted me across the street. He saw me with my friends and came over to me on the corner with his manager and shook my hand. Lucky said, "How are you doing, Tony?"

"Great, Lucky. Are you ready for the fight?"

He said, "I am always ready. Are you going to see me fight?"

I said, "I will be there Lucky."

He said, "Okay, but buy the tickets from me because I get a cut of the tickets I sell."

"Sure thing, Lucky."

"You guys take care," he said to the gang, adding to me, "Tony, I will see you tomorrow in the gym."

After he left, my friends' mouths were open they said, "Wow, you know Lucky!" I could see they were really excited that Lucky came over to talk with us. All of the guys from Left's gym always took time to talk to you when they saw you on the street. It was as if you were a part of the family.

I went to see Lucky fight at Jersey City High School, where he fought this older man. Lucky knocked him out in the second round with a right hand. Lucky's face was red because the guy hit him a couple of times, but you could see Lucky concentrating and waiting on the time to throw his right hand. They raised Lucky's arms in victory and the crowd was going nuts. Lucky's manager cut off the tape on his boxing gloves and took the gloves off. Lucky threw the boxing gloves into the crowd.

Lucky was beating everyone in New Jersey. He had a fight with a boxer who was ranked fifth in the world. I didn't get to see it because the fight was an hour away from Jersey City and I couldn't get a ride, but I saw an article about it in the newspaper. The fight was called a draw and Lucky was mad because he thought he won the fight. He said he was robbed in his own backyard by the boxing judges.

One Friday night I was at this all-night house party when I heard the doorbell ring. One of the girls told me Jake was at the door for me. It was about 2 AM. I went outside and said, "What's up, Jake?"

"Have you heard the news?"

"What news?"

"Lucky got shot in the head," he said.

"Oh, man, how did it happen?"

"I don't know, but it is on the news," he said.

I was praying for Lucky but the next day he died. *The Jersey Journal's* headline read, "Prince of Jersey City Dead." The paper said Lucky had committed suicide. I do not know what really happened; all I knew was that it was a shame. Lucky had a great future ahead of him and now it was over. I was really hurt because Lucky had been so nice to me. My heart really hurt bad.

Lucky was a special guy. I think Lucky fought to earn the love he felt when he was boxing. He got treated like a prince because he mastered boxing and he was nice to his fans. After he beat the crap out of me sparring, he always told me, "Nobody ever said it is going to be easy, kid." Every time I get down or something is not working out for me, I think of Lucky and how he said, "No one said it would be easy," and how hard he worked. Lucky always told me, "Wait until you fight somebody your own age; you are going to beat the crap out of them."

Maybe Lucky worked too hard or maybe he needed a break to have a good time. He worked out all year long and he had a lot of pressure on him. All of his friends would go to see him fight and he felt like he was fighting for his friends and family when his stepped into the ring.

Patty and I took the bus to see Lucky at the wake. We walked in the funeral home and it was full of people, with Lucky in the casket. Lucky had a big family and they were devastated. They all looked like they were in shock. Patty and I paid our respects to his family and walked up to the casket to say our prayers. I knelt down by Lucky with Patty kneeling next to me. I was praying and I was looking at Lucky, and I just could not believe he was dead. We finished praying and I touched Lucky's arm. I said, "I am going to miss you, Lucky, but I will never forget you."

We went to pay our respects his father. Lefty was at the funeral home and he told Lucky's father that Patty and I were two boxers. I told Lucky's father I was sorry for his loss. The funeral home was packed. Over two thousand people attended Lucky's funeral. I don't think he ever made too many enemies. Even after he beat the crap out of somebody in the ring, he was nice to them after the fight.

I started to spar with Ray, a tough light heavyweight that fought for the world championship. Ray beat a former world champ. I really liked him because he was a happy fellow out of the ring. He had trouble making weight for the light heavy-weight division so he wore a plastic bag under his shirt so he would sweat to lose weight. Ray was funny out of the ring but in the ring, he was all business. I would think as a kid, *How can these guy talk and joke with you and then get you in the ring and try to kill you?* That is the way it was; fighting was their business. Ray always told me, "I want to retire young. I like to eat and I like the women, and when you are training for a fight you can't have either one of those things."

I had my first boxing match in front of a crowd on the USS Lexington, a Navy ship dry-docked in Bayonne, New Jersey. We went there to put a show on for the sailors. We had to go on the Navy base on a bus and the MPs had to get on the bus to check us out. As soon as we got on the boat, I had to go to the bathroom to take a pee. I was watching the guy next to me piss on his boxing boots and I was laughing. My boxing coach, Paul, said, "What the hell are you laughing at, you? You are pissing on your boots, too." The sailors were a great audience; they love to see the fights. I was boxing with this tall kid from Left's Gym, and Lefty told us to just move. He said, "Don't kill each other; it is just an exhibition."

The kid and I got in the ring and the sailors were going nuts. They had proba-bly been out on the ship for awhile and they were ready for some entertainment. The bell rang for the first round and I was ready to just move with this kid, but he hit me with three hard shots, I decided to screw the exhibition garbage and I went after him. Whenever somebody connected with a punch, the crowed went nuts. I was determined not to let this kid get the best of me. I was not in great shape because of my smoking so I was huffing and puffing. The kid was hitting me pretty good. I was usually a good defensive fighter because I had to be careful sparring with the pros, but all I learned in the gym went out the window when I got mad. I started to connect with my right hand and was rocking the kid. I guess all of my time watching Lucky pivot when he threw his right hand paid off. In the third round I started to nail him good with right hands. The sailors were going nuts. They started shouting, "Knock him out!" They had to stop the match a little early because the kid's legs started to wobble. It was only an exhibition but we were going at it.

After the match, I was mad at myself because I did not box like I did in the gym. I just went after the kid and got hit too much. I was not thinking about defense, I was just thinking about punching the kid. I was afraid because Lefty had told me that some guys fought great in the gym but they could not fight in front of a crowd. After the fight Jake, Patty, and Chubs were waiting for me with a six-pack. I drank a beer and had a cigarette, but the next day was a school day so we did not party a lot. I knew I had to stop smoking if I wanted to be a good boxer.

When I got to the gym the next day, Lefty said, "What happening to the take it easy and moving around?"

I said, "Lefty, the kid nailed me and I had to fight."

He said, Yeah, I know, they told me you did good."

The next time I was supposed to fight, I was serious because I wanted to make sure I boxed did not brawl like I had on the Navy ship. I was not talking and Lefty did not like me too be serious because he thought I got too nervous. This other boxer, Tom, was going with us to fight. Tom was nuts; he loved to fight but it seemed liked he was high on something because he was asking Lefty a lot of questions. He asked Lefty if he had a lot of girls when he was young. Lefty said, "No, I didn't, but we used to go to this dime-a-dance place. You would pay the girls a dime and they would slow dance with you." He said, "The girls knew how to touch your pecker just right when they were dancing with you to make you cum in your pants." Once I heard that I could not stop laughing. I could not be serious any longer. I kept trying to be serious and I kept thinking of Lefty with the dime-a-dance girls and I would start laughing. We got to the school where the fight was and they did not have anyone in my weight class so I did not get to fight that night.

Lefty would ride me home at night after I was finished working out. He would have me check the gym to make sure nobody was hiding there. He was always nervous about someone hiding in the gym. I thought, *Lefty, what the hell, do you think somebody is going to hide in the gym to hit the heavy bag all night?* But I never said anything out loud. Riding home with him was a treat. He was nuts. If someone parked too close to him and he had a hard time getting out of the parking place, he would say to me, "Watch this; I am going to teach them not to park so close to me." He would start ramming the cars in front and behind him with his bumper. Each time we rammed the car our heads would snap and he said, "That will teach them, don't you think?" I just laughed.

Once we got on the road, Lefty started talking about the people we passed. He said, "See those kids over there? They are junkies. You see that lady over there? She is a whore." I do not even know if Lefty knew these people but I always enjoyed my rides home with him because I laughed the whole way. He had a wealth of knowledge in boxing, too. He did not teach you a lot but what he told you was very important. He knew that boxing was an art and you had to develop many of the skills on your own. Lefty made sure you pivoted when you threw a right hand. He said that was very important; it made the difference between hitting someone and knocking them out. Lefty told me boxing was like going to war—you had to be ready for anything. He said, "You have to be smarter and have better skills than your opponent. When you hit them, you have to hurt them."

I started to get in to a lot of street fights. After fighting professional boxers, hard guys in the street were fun to fight with. It did not take a lot for me to get into a fight with somebody; they just had to say something bad to me or look at me like they wanted to fight. There were many tough guys in Jersey City that were always looking for a fight. Usually on the street, I fought more than one guy at a time. One night I was out with all the guys from Thirty-three Schoolyard when we went to this club where we were dancing and drinking and having a great time. It was getting late and I got into Jake's into car and he said, "Let's go to this other club." I said okay. We had to park a few blocks from the club because it was packed. Jake parked the car and I got out. I did not know that Jake was not behind me; he was taking a piss by the car and I was walking towards the club, singing. These three guys who were crossing the street stopped and started staring at me. I knew they wanted to fight and I looked for Jake but he was not there. I said to myself, *Screw it, there are only three of them.* I ran over and hit the biggest one of the guys with a right hand and knocked him down with one punch. I got on top of him and started punching him in the face. One of his friends kicked me in the face. I got knocked out for few seconds, but when I got up, Jake was there. All of the guys had run away. They knew Jake and were afraid he was going to beat them up. I said, "Let's get them!" Jake got the one kid that I was punching in the face and brought him over to me.

He said, "You two make friends." Both of us were bloody but we shock hands and it was over. Jake told me he did not want to start a gang war over some stupid crap. He told me he had to take me to the hospital because my lip was ripped open, but I told him I did not want to go to the hospital. He took me to a mirror and showed me my lip. It was hanging off my face and I knew I had to go. We went to the hospital and they stitched up my face.

When I got back to gym on Monday, Lefty asked me what had happened and I told him I got jumped by three guys. Lefty looked at me and said, "If you want to fight like that, you might as well get paid for it." Lefty was right—if I got paid for all the times I fought in the street, I would have been rich. I could not spar with the stitches in my face but I got up the next day to do my roadwork. I ran three miles. I was immune from pain. I felt it a little but I did not let it bother me. A few weeks later I was in this club and I saw this girl, Kate, I knew from grammar school. I knew Kate's boyfriend who was not in the club. We were talking about old times in St. Richard's School and she was asking me about Jake when she said, "I heard you are going to fight in the Golden Gloves."

This guy came over to us and started to try and pick her up while I was talking to her. I told the guy I knew her boyfriend and he should leave her alone. This guy was older and told me, "I learned a long time ago when a boyfriend is not around, you don't worry about him." As the guy turned around, I punched him right off his stool. Within seconds bouncers came from everywhere. One of them kicked me in the face but I did not see which one. I got a black eye from the kick. By the time I had gotten up the manager was there; I guess the bouncers did not want me one-on-one because they were nowhere to be found. I just told the manager, "Well, I think I should be leaving now."

"That's a good idea," he said. I walked outside and Kate and her friend were waiting for me to give me a ride home. When my mother saw me she said, "Oh, my God, you are going to get killed."

I told her, "Don't worry about it, Ma."

Chapter Seventeen:

Saying Goodbye to Grandma

The next day my mother and I went to see my grandmother, who was dying in a hospital in New York. I loved my grandmother and wanted to see her as much as I could before she died so I went to see her every weekend. They brought this black lady to stay in the room with her. The first week they brought her in, this lady looked like she was going to die. The next week I went to see my grandmother and her companion looked great. She and Grandma were singing songs and the lady was happy. I said, "Wow, Grandma, this lady looks great. I thought she was going to die."

Grandma looked at me and said, "All she needed was a little love." Grandma knew everything about her companion, from her kids to her husband to where she lived.

My mother and I were talking to Grandma and Grandma kept looking at my black eye. She told my mother to go get some napkins in the bathroom. My mother went in the bathroom and said, "I can't find any napkins."

"Close the bathroom door and keep looking for napkins until I tell you to come out!" Grandma said. Then she looked at me and said, "Come here, you."

I went over to her and she held my arm. She asked me if I was fighting over a girl. I said, "No, Grandma."

She grabbed me by the shirt and said, "Don't bull crap your grandma. Tony, don't fight over girls—there are too many of them to fight over." She said, "You never win fighting over girls." She told me there were a lot of things worth fighting over but girls were not one of them.

"I'll remember, Grandma," I said.

I went to see my Grandma every week because I loved to listen to her great wisdom. She told me that love was the strongest power and the more love you gave, the more you received. She said that there were a lot of bad people in the world and that a lot of people did not have the balls to do the right things. She said, "Tony, you got balls; you always do the right thing." She said, "God watches everything you do and if you do the right thing, you don't have anything to worry about." My grandma told me she was not afraid to die. She said, "I lived a good life. I have had a lot of joy in my life and I did the right thing. I am ready to go with God when he calls me."

My grandma was the best person I ever knew in my life. She always did the right thing no matter who she pissed off. When she died, I was not sad. She knew it was coming and she went to be with God. I missed her but I know I will see her again. My grandmother taught me a lot of important lessons and I always listened to her. My mother was sad but she had a great faith in God, too, and she knew that her mother had gone to a better life.

Chapter Eighteen:

Trouble

It was 1978, a Friday night, and I was getting ready to go out. I had taken a bath, so I put on some disco music to listen to while I dried my hair. My mother knew that when I got ready to go out there was a good chance I was going to get in trouble. Before I left my room, I looked in the mirror and said to myself, "There is a fifty/fifty chance you are going to get into a fight tonight." That was just a part of living in the city and not taking any crap from anybody. You see, I had a choice—I could have stayed in the house, or I could have walked away from fights, but at this time in my life, I thought I was doing the right thing. I was taught from the time I was a little boy that if somebody messes with you, the right thing to do is stand up for yourself.

All this while, the music was blasting and I was singing and having a good old time when my mother turned off the radio. She looked at me and said, "You got to do something for me tonight."

I said, "What, Ma?"

"Don't get into a fight tonight."

"I'll try not to."

"Don't get in a fight tonight because I can't take it right now." I knew she was afraid I was going to get killed in a street fight. She was still sad about my grandma and I had to respect my mother's wishes.

I finished getting dressed, I kissed my mother goodbye, and I told her don't worry about me. I walked up to Mulligan's Lounge to see who was hanging out but all I could think of was, *I got to stay out of trouble tonight.* When I got to Mulligan's, a friend of mine, Eddie, was hanging out. Eddie asked me if I wanted a beer and I said yes. He asked me what my plans were and I said, "I don't know, but I don't want to hang around here tonight."

"I do not feel like hanging around here tonight, either. I got a full tank of gas in my car," he said.

"Want to take a ride to my father's trailer up in the mountains?" I figured I could not get into too much trouble in the mountains.

He said, "Let's go," so I brought a case of beer and we headed to my father's trailer. Eddie was pulled over for speeding as we went up the mountain, but since he was in the National Guard, the police gave him a break. We spent the whole night talking and drinking. It was a boring night but I was doing the best I could to stay out of a fight. After a few hours at the trailer, we headed back to Jersey City and Eddie got stopped by the same cops for weaving. They asked Eddie if he could drive safe and he said, "Yes, I will be all right," so they let us go. On the ride, back I was thinking, *This is good. My mother will be happy I stayed out of a fight tonight.*

As soon as Eddie drove into Jersey City, this guy cut him off.

Eddie got pissed but I told him to let the guy go.

"Okay," he said, slowing down so the guy could pass us but when we slowed down, the guy slowed down. The guy waited for Eddie and cut him off again.

I said, "Eddie leave the guy go."

Eddie was pissed, and the guy cut him off again. "I can't take this crap!" he said.

"Okay, Eddie," I said. "Pull over."

We got out of the car. The other car stopped and two guys jumped out. One was a big guy and the other was a Chinese guy. The big guy had a big mouth and told Eddie he was going to beat the crap out of him. Now, Eddie did not doing anything at all to this guy. This guy thought he was a hard guy and he was going to beat us up. I was not afraid of the big guy, but all I could think of was, *Great, I bet this Chinese guy knows Kung Fu or some kind of martial arts.* That thought did not last long because the big guy ran over to Eddie and punched him in the face. As soon as I saw the guy hit Eddie, I went after him and hit him with a right hand to the jaw and he went down on the street. I jumped on him, but I was watching the Chinese guy. I punched the big guy in the face, saying, "You made me break a promise I made to my mother!"

The Chinese dude did not do anything, but then a car stopped on the other side of the street and the big guy's friends were coming over to us. I was still on top of him and I had to think quick because I did not want to get kicked in the face again. So I bit the big guy on the check and told him, "Tell your friends to get back in the car or I am going to bite your cheek off." One of his friends came over and asked if he was okay.

The big guy said, "Yes, I am fine, get back in the car."

I held on to the guy's throat and said, "If you ever cut me or my friends off again, I will kill you." I let him up and he ran to his car and drove away. Eddie and I got back in his car and he drove me home. All I could think of is that you were not going to find any peace in Jersey City. You had to make a choice if you were going to be abused or take care of yourself. I did not keep my promise to my mother, but I did not have a scratch on me. I got in the house and my mother asked me if I had gotten into a fight. I just said, "Do you see any black eyes?"

She said no, and I said, "I love you, Ma. Go to sleep."

I tried to stay out of trouble but I could not say no to a fight. If I saw a hard guy and he wanted to fight, I fought. I was taught as a kid not to back out of a fight. I boxed every day with professionals, so fighting a regular guy was nothing. I liked to fight more than one guy at a time on the street but I usually got my butt kicked, which, to me, was just a learning experience making me a better fighter. Anybody could beat one guy, but it took a lot of skill to fight three guys at a time. A lot of boxers get into trouble because they really don't learn how to leave the fighting in the ring. The real tough guys took care of business better than fighting in the street.

My friend Robbie got stabbed; I asked him where the guy hung out so I could take care of him. Robbie said, "Don't worry about it; my father's got a friend that is a cop and they got the guy and threw him in with the biggest dude in the jail. That guy is going to be walking like he rides horses for the rest of his life." That was the smart way to do it but I did not have the patience. You need a strategy to take care of business without fighting in the street.

A lot of my friends went to a public high school in Jersey City, so on the days I did not have school I would go hang out with them outside the school. Public school was a joke. Most of my friends did not graduate; they had to go back to night school because they would drink beer instead of going to school. I loved to hang out with them but I knew that not going to school would catch up with them. Some of my friends would go to classes if they liked the teacher, or if the teachers reported them absent because they didn't want to get expelled from school. But most of the day they just drank beer.

Jake started to go out with this girl, Mary, whom he really liked. One day he saw Mary get into a car with this guy from school and Jake jumped on the hood of the car and punched a hole through the windshield and beat the guy up. The whole time Jake was beating the guy up, Mary was telling him that he was just a friend and he was just riding her home. Jake busted up his hand pretty good and busted up the guy pretty good. He found out latter that he was related to the guy and he had to pay to get the car fixed. He felt bad about beating the guy up but he said, "You never know if someone is being nice to your girlfriend or if they are going to try to pick up your girlfriend." I don't think anybody tried to drive Jake's girlfriend home from school after that.

I broke my leg playing basketball. It was tough having a cast on my legs because I could not run from the cops. We were all drinking down at Thirty-three Schoolyard one night when we heard the cop siren. When I looked around, everybody was gone and there was beer everywhere. I knew I could not run, so I just stayed there and kept drinking my beer. The cops were chasing somebody else. My friends came back and said that they were sorry, but it was just a natural reaction to run from the cops. If you ran as soon as you heard or saw them, you usually did not get caught.

The next day we were having a ring ceremony in school and afterwards I was hanging out with my friends from high school drinking beer in a park. We were all going to a party that night so Paul and Shawn said, "We will walk you home and then we can all go to the party together." We started walking to my house and who do I see but my friend Stanley speeding down the street in his red Charger.

When he saw me he pulled over and said, "Tony, do you and your friends want a ride?" I said sure, but as soon as we got in the car Stanley said, "I have to make a stop before I take you home. I have to go over New York to get an Easter bunny for my girl." I knew Stanley was not going to get no Easter bunny in New York. As soon as I saw the neighborhood we drove to, I knew he was going to get high on heroin. I did not want to say anything to my friends from school because I knew they would be scared.

New York City was only a fifteen-minute drive. Stanley stopped in this rundown neighborhood, jumped out of the car, and said, "I will be right back."

Paul and Shawn said, "He is not getting a bunny here."

"He is getting high," I said. They asked if he was buying heroin and I said yes.

"Oh, crap," Shawn said.

"Don't worry; it don't take effect until a half hour and we will be at my house by then."

Stanley came out of the apartment building rubbing his nose and with his arm bleeding. Stanley got in the car and Paul asked him how long it would take before he got high. Stanley said, "Crap, I am feeling it already," and he hit the gas. I looked in the rearview mirror to see Paul and Shawn were as white as ghosts. Stanley was speeding through red lights, but all my friends drove nuts and I was never afraid because I trusted them with my life. We got home safe and sound and Stanley said, "I will see you around."

Paul and Shawn got out of the car and said, "Thank God!"

I was never afraid with any of my friends—I guess I had faith in all of them—but God had to send us angels to protect us or we would have been dead. We went to the party and had a good time.

Chapter Nineteen:

The Golden Gloves

Jake, Patty, and I all signed up to fight in the New Jersey Golden Gloves competition in 1978, when I was eighteen years old. We had to get pictures taken so me and Jake went to one of those booths that take your photo. I had stitches in my lip from a street fight.

We were all working out hard, but I figured if anybody had a chance to win the Golden Gloves it was Patty. He was a real good boxer and he fought in the lightweight class. The Golden Gloves matches were fought in Elizabeth, New Jersey. It was a rough crowd. Many New Jersey boxers went to fight in the New York Gloves, but Lefty said we didn't have a chance to win there unless we knocked everybody out, because they wouldn't give a Jersey boy a decision.

The Elizabeth crowd was so rough that Lefty would not go to the Golden Gloves fights. He said, "I am too old for that crap." He sent us to the fight with other trainers from the gym. It was November. The first night we were supposed to fight, we showed up to the armory in Elizabeth. We all waited nervously in the dressing room to see who we were going to fight. This man came in to the dressing room and told us we were not going to fight that night because the lighter weight classes were going to box. Patty weighed a hundred and six pounds and only had five guys in his weight class so he did not have to fight that night, either. We watched some of the matches, and I was keeping track of what boxers did well and what mistakes they were making. I knew I had to stay focused and stick to a game plan of boxing and not slugging.

When I went to work out on Saturday morning, Lefty said, "I heard you guys did not fight." Lefty said, "Sometimes you have to wait. They have many boxers in some of the weight classes and they will eliminate some of them in the weight classes that are crowded." The Golden Gloves were single elimination—if you lost one fight, you were out of the tournament. We kept training and one night in the beginning of January, 1979, Lefty received a phone call in the gym office. When he came out of his office he told Patty, Jake, and I we would be fighting Friday night.

Paulie and Mr. Weaver were the coaches that were going to work our corners. Patty, Patty's dad, and I drove down to the fights together. Patty's dad asked me if I was scared, and I said, "I'm not scared of fighting, but I am scared of losing." I did not want to get my butt kicked in front of all my friends.

Patty's dad said, "Listen, you are the one getting in the ring and all your friends are on the outside of the ring. You are the one with the balls—if you win or lose, you had the balls to get in there, and that means a lot." That made me feel better but I still wanted to win the fight so my friends would be proud of me.

As soon as I got out of the car in Elizabeth, I saw my friends waiting for us. Anthony came up to me and said, "Do not worry about nothing but fighting, but there is a shotgun in the trunk just in case we have a problem over here."

Jake drove his own car down to the fight. He did not look good. I asked him if he was sick and he said he had the flu.

"You sure you want to fight with the flu, Jake?"

He said, "Yeah, I worked too hard not to fight." I gave Jake a lot of credit for fighting with the flu.

Patty fought in the first match of the night and won a decision. He looked good up there. Then they called the light heavyweights. We all went into a room and they matched us up. I stayed away from Jake because I did not want to fight him. They match me up with a white guy the same size as me, and they matched Jake up with this big black guy. It felt like we were gladiators; you were being matched up to do battle in front of the crowd. I was thinking, *Box as you boxed in the gym, don't get mad.* Jake fought first. He got stopped in the first round; he probably should not have fought with the flu because it was hard enough fighting healthy—but like Patty's father said, he had the balls to get in there and had nothing to be ashamed of. I was proud of Jake.

He came over to me and said, "You go get them." They came into the locker room and told me I was fighting next. I got up and started to loosen up. Patty came in the locker room with a gold medal of Jesus' head. He said, "Kiss this for good luck," and I kissed it. When they called me, I did not look at the crowd. I just walked into the ring. I kept saying to myself, *Box and don't get hit and don't get mad.* The Elizabeth Armory was packed; I did not look for any of my friends in the crowd. I was focused on boxing well.

The guy I was fighting was easy to hit. During the first round, I was jabbing and moving so well I don't think the guy hit me once. The bell rang and I went back to my corner. Paulie said, "Listen, you are doing good. That guy is dropping his left hand. When he drops his left hand, you hit him with a right hand." It is funny—I was so focused all I saw was the guy; I knew what punches he was going to throw before he threw them. I was hitting the guy with jabs, and then he dropped his left hand. I threw a right and knocked him down. As soon as he got up, I just kept throwing punches until the ref stopped the fight.

All my friends were going nuts. It felt good to win but I knew I had to fight again soon and I knew it could be me getting knocked out then. Chucky and Chubs bet money on me and won. I hung out with my friends for a while, drank a six-pack of beer, and went home.

I was working out shadow boxing in Left's and this guy Bobby, who was a professional boxer from the gym, said, "Are your friends going to be at the fight Friday?" When I said yes, he said, "We like when your friends go to the fight because they are crazy."

The time I fought this big black guy from Bayonne, New Jersey. I knew his manager, Rutty, who trained at Left's and helped guys train in Bayonne. Rutty was a tough Irish boxer who could stay in there with the best of them. The guy from Bayonne was about six inches taller than me and had long arms. He was solid muscle. I knew I was going to have to hit this big guy with right hands because his arms were two long for me to jab with him. I really did not want to get into a slugfest but I had to develop a strategy quickly to deal with this tall, strong boxer.

The bell rang and we both went to the center of the ring. I threw a jab, and he threw a left hook over my jab and almost took my head off. I thought, *Screw the jabs, they are not going to work because he has the reach advantage on me.* I did not want to get caught with one of his left hooks. I started throwing right hands and left hooks. The first round was tough as we both traded hard punches. The bell rang and when I went back to the corner, Mr. Weaver slapped me in the head. He said, "You have to move your head." He had a white towel and he said, "Put your head down in the towel and take a deep breath through your nose." He had a little bottle under the towel. I do not know what it was but it gave me a head rush. The bell rang to start the second round and I got up from the stool and thought, *Great, now I have to fight this big guy with a buzz.*

The head rush ended and I felt fresh. We were hitting each other good. I knocked him down with a right hand and though, *Oh, please, God, let him stay down.* He was a tough guy. He got up and was still strong, throwing a lot of punches. Paulie and Mr. Weaver were yelling at me to keep throwing punches. Every time the guy started throwing a lot of punches, I kept my hands up so the guy could not hurt me, but I knew I'd better start throwing punches if I didn't want the ref to stop the fight. The guy had a good second round; he was throwing a lot of punches, but I was nailing him, too. I went back to the corner and Mr. Weaver was yelling at me. I sat down on the stool and he gave me a slap on the cheek to wake me up; he hit harder than the boxers, but he really wanted me to win.

The third round started and I started nailing the guy pretty good. I hit him with a right hand and sent him flying back to the corner of the ring. It was like everything was in slow motion. As soon as I hit him, I saw him flying back into the corner and blood was flying out of his nose. His blood was flying up in the air and he landed on his butt when he hit the canvas. He was sitting on his butt in the corner with blood all over his face and I started smiling. He had put up a good fight but now he was mine. I was smiling and thinking, *Now I got him.* I knew he was done. He got up, but he lost his strength. I hit him with another right hand and it knocked him down. The referee stopped the fight.

I gave the guy a lot of credit; he was a real tough boxer. I got a black eye from the fight and all I could think of was, *Great, I have to fight next week with a black eye.* Rutty, my opponent's manager, came over to me and said, "That was a tough fight; the kid hung in there pretty good."

I said, "Yeah, Rutty, he is a tough guy."

People started to take notice of me. A lot of boxers fight in the Golden Gloves and lose their first fight, but when you win your second fight, they know you have a chance to become the Golden Glove Champ. My attitude was that I would try my best; if I lose, I lose, but I got on my knees and prayed every night that I won the Golden Gloves.

You can become close to God when you box because when you are fighting, nobody can help you. You train hard and use your skills, but you are alone with your opponent in the ring and only God can help you. I went to church every Sunday and asked God to let me become the Golden Glove Champ. I always prayed that I did not get hurt bad and I did not hurt my opponent bad. The beautiful thing about God is that he is always there to help you when nobody else can.

Friday came fast and I had to fight again. I put twenty dollars in my pocket before I left my house. The twenty bucks was for a case of beer if I lost the fight. If I lost, I was going to celebrate because I tried my best. I had not drunk more then a six-pack of beer in three months. I was working hard so as soon as the

Golden Gloves was over, I was going to party. I was down to the semi-finals; if I won this fight at least I would get to the finals. If you lost in the finals, you got a silver glove. It was nothing like getting the Golden Glove, but it was a great accomplishment. There were only four of us left: two black guys and two white guys. There was a tall white boxer and a tall black boxer. The color did not matter; I wanted to fight the smaller boxer so I could use my jab. There was a stocky black boxer. I wanted to fight him. The other white boxer and black guy were too tall. I did not want a war like I had had the week before. I wanted to box. Mr. Weaver told me they were going to match me up with the shorter boxer because they wanted me to fight Butler in the finals.

Jake Butler, the tall black boxer, was the favorite to win the Golden Gloves. He had knockouts in all of his matches. The tall white boxer and Butler fought first. The tall white boxer put up a good fight but Butler knocked him out in the second round. I was watching Butler. He was big, and he kept throwing punches at his opponent. I knew the only way to stop him was to nail him with a right hand. I felt tired that night. I usually went to bed about 10 PM and it was about 10:30 so I was fighting after my bedtime. I felt good about fighting the smaller opponent because I knew I could use my jab.

A man came in the dressing room and said, "You two are fighting next, get ready." I started to warm up outside the dressing room. I could see that more of my friends were at the fight than ever before. The bell rang and the other guy came right at me. We started fighting and I knew right away that this guy was tougher than he looked. I was nailing him with hard punches but I was not hurting him. I knocked his mouthpiece out but he kept fighting. My jab was working pretty well. I would hit him with punches and dance away so he could not hit me. He liked to fight inside so when he started throwing punches to my body, I traded punches with him on the inside. I was nailing him with upper cuts and left hooks inside. At the end of the first round he hit me after the bell. I did not even feel the punch but it pissed my friends off; they were trying to jump into the ring to get to the boxer. It could have been an honest mistake. It was just a part of the game.

I went back to the corner. Mr. Weaver was not in my corner that night because he had to go to his son's Navy graduation. I sure missed him and his little bottle that night because I was tired. I guess I was getting to the point of over-training because I hadn't taken a break for three months. Paulie said, "This guy is tough. It is a close fight, so you got to throw more punches than him." I was tired, but I knew I had to keep busy to win this fight.

We traded a lot of punches in the second round. Hollywood was at ringside rooting for me. He kept saying, "You get off first." Hollywood knew it was a close fight and I had to stay busy or I would lose. The boxer had a good left hook but I could see it coming. He nailed me with the left hook good only one time. He was a strong boxer and I knew I could not take many of those left hooks. So I moved back when I saw the hook coming. He hit me below the belt once and I could hear my friends yelling at him and coming up to the ring as if they wanted to jump in and help me. They were used to jumping in at street fights, but I was all alone with this boxer. I knew he did not try to punch me low; he was trying to punch my stomach. We had big cups to protect our groins so the low punch did not even bother me.

The bell rang to end the second round and I sat on the stool. I was sleepy. I was in good shape but I was tired. I was not physically tired, I was sleepy tired. I had a hard time staying awake. I knew I had to wake myself up because Mr. Weaver was not there. The bell rang for the third and final round and I knew I had to score some points. I hit this boxer with hard shots and knew I was not going to knock him out.

We went out for the third round and the referee said, "Keep it clean; you guys are putting on a real good show." As soon as I got to the center of the ring, I hit my opponent with two jabs. I could feel the crowd cheering every time I threw a punch so I kept throwing jabs. I was snapping his head back with every jab. I was trying to hit this boxer with more punches then he hit me. It was a great fight and the fans were going nuts. The bell rang and as I shook hands with the boxer, he said, "You are tough."

I said, "You too, good fight."

The fight went to the judges—this fight could go either way. The fair thing was to call a draw but they did not have draws in the Golden Gloves.

The whole time the judges were scoring, my friends were chanting, "Tony, Tony." The referee called both of us to the center of the ring. I was praying that I got the decision. The announcer said, "The winner, in the blue corner, from Jersey City, Tony."

My friends were going nuts. The other boxer was pissed, but I hugged him and said, "Great fight." I felt bad for him because I knew the fight could have gone either way, but I was happy because I knew I had made it to the finals and I would at least win a silver glove. But I knew I had to fight Butler, and I knew he could kill me.

Hollywood came up to me as soon as I got out of the ring. "Good fight, kid! He was a good, tough boxer and you would have lost if you had not traded punches with him." It felt good that Hollywood told me it was a good fight because I knew he had seen a lot of good fights in his time. All of my friends won money on the fight so they were proud of me, and that was the most important thing to me.

Most guys go in the Golden Gloves to prove something to themselves and get respect from people. Patty and I made it to the Golden Glove finals.—two boys from Jersey City and from Thirty-three Schoolyard made it to the New Jersey Golden Glove finals. Everyone from Lefty's was excited. I did more praying that week than ever before in my life. I knew everybody thought Butler was going to kick my butt. I have to admit if I had had to make a bet on the fight, I would have bet on him, too. However, I learned from boxing that trying your best is all that matters. If you can look at yourself in the mirror and say, "I gave it everything I had," then you have to be proud of yourself.

I was working out at the gym for the final fight when my friends Anthony and Chucky came up to the gym to see me. The way we grew up was that when one of us was in a fight, we were all in the fight. I know all our friends wanted to help Patty and me. However, this was a fair fight and my friends were not used to fair fights; they were used to street fights where all your friends jumped in if you were losing. Patty and I were on our own for these fights. The only one that could help us was God. I wish Anthony had boxed. He was tough and he loved to fight. Anthony told me, "They got too many rules in boxing." He came close to me and said, "I have to talk to you"

I said, "Go ahead, Anthony."

"Listen, I have been watching this guy Butler, and he likes to back people up." He said, "Don't back up. When he comes in, stay there and fight and don't back up."

I said, "I was thinking the same thing. I know I can't box with this guy; I got to hurt him."

Anthony said, "Don't back up."

"Okay, Anthony," I said. "Listen, Anthony, tell all the guys not to bet on me Friday night because I don't know if I can beat this guy."

"Don't worry about nothing but the fight. If you lose, you tried your best and we are still proud of you."

"Thanks, Anthony."

Chucky said, "Knock him out, Tony," and I said I would try my best.

Anthony was not a boxer but he was a great street fighter and all great fighters have strategies. I knew I could not let Butler back me up.

I was sparring with Rodell, a pro that had fought many world champions. He usually took it easy on me when we were sparring but Lefty told him I had a tough fight coming up so he put the pressure on me. Rodell and I were going at it good. I would always try to throw more punches than him because I knew it could make the difference between winning and losing. Rodell, like most fighters from Jersey City, worked all day and then fought at night. Rodell was a tough club fighter and he had a tough life working in the factory all day and fighting at night. I really loved Rodell; he was nice to me. We beat each other up every day in the gym, but I respected him. I really gave it to him, boxing and working to take care of his family. I knew I did not want his life, but I gave him a lot of credit. I liked all the fighters from Left's, but Rodell was special to me.

The night before the Golden Glove finals, Lefty had me shadow box and warm up. He gave me a rubdown that night and said, "Listen, just give it all you got. You cannot do nothing else."

I knew everybody in the gym thought Butler was going to knock me out. Butler had all knockouts; I had two knockouts and one decision. I did not worry about the fight because I knew all I could do was my best. Either way, after this fight, I was going to party—if I was still alive.

The night of the Golden Gloves finals I was getting ready to leave my house and my mother asked me if I was scared. I told her the same thing I'd said before: "I am not scared of fighting. I am just scared of losing." I was not scared of dying. I knew it was part of the game that you could get killed boxing. Although I was not scared, I knew Butler could kill me. I figured I'd rather get killed doing something I like—after all, you could get killed crossing the street.

My mother said, "Listen, I feel bad that I am not going to see you fight but if you started getting your butt kicked I would have to jump in the ring and help you."

"Ma, it is better you don't go to see me fight because sometimes it looks like we are hurt. We bleed, but we are not hurt—but people that are not in the boxing game panic when they see blood. I have to worry about the boxer I am fighting and I do not want to think that you are worrying about me." I told her, "Believe me, I got enough problems worrying about the guy I am fighting."

She kissed me and said, "Break a leg." She never said "good luck" because she thought that was bad luck. I told her I loved her, put the twenty bucks in my pocket, and left for the fight.

I met Patty halfway to Left's Gym. I did not like to talk before my fights but Patty was nervous and he had to talk. Whatever Patty said, I just said yes. We saw this dog and the dog started howling and we both started laughing. Patty told me he had run ten miles in the morning. I said that was not smart and he said, "Yes, I know, but I was so nervous I had to run."

I just said, "Okay, it is over; just think about your fight."

We got to the gym and Paulie and Mr. Weaver were waiting for us. I was glad to see Mr. Weaver because I knew I was going to need that little bottle tonight. I went up to see Lefty and he said, "Give them hell, Tony." We left the gym to start our journey to Elizabeth. Three white kids made it to the Golden Gloves finals. The other boxers were black or Hispanic. Color meant nothing—when the bell rang you had your brains, heart, and soul. Those are the only things that matter in the ring. Boxing fans make a big thing about black, white, and Hispanics fighting each other. I guess it is like a uniform to most people; if you have the same color jersey as the fighter, then you cheer that fighter. I loved boxing because nothing mattered inside the ring except your skills, guts, and your soul. I loved all the fighters that I fought; it is kind of pouring your heart out for someone. You get to see your opponent's heart and he gets to see yours. I always respected anyone that had the guts to get in the rings. So when they said there were only three white guys in the finals it did not matter to me. I knew you would get to see a little bit of the soul and the heart of the fighters and that is more important. Color does not mean anything.

Patty fought the first fight of the night. I said, "Good luck, Patty." I knew Patty would do great because he was a great boxer. I was relaxing in the dressing room and Robbie, a friend of mine, came in the dressing room. Robbie said, "Patty is in a tough fight."

I sat by the door watching the fight and I told Robbie, "Don't worry about it; Patty is going to wear this guy out in the third round." By the third round, I was getting nervous—Patty had his hands full, and the kid he was fighting was the Junior Olympic Champ of New Jersey. This kid had sixty amateur fights; Patty had had only two amateur fights before this one. Patty whacked this kid with a left hook and I said, "That is it; Patty has him." Patty hit the kid so hard with the hook he knocked him off his feet but the kid landed right back on his feet and kept fighting. Nobody had as much energy as Patty—he had run ten miles in the morning and now he was fighting. Patty lost a close decision, but the kid threw more punches than he did. Patty came back to the locker room drinking a soda and was as happy as he could be. His nose was swollen, he had a black eye, and he had a huge smile on his face. I hugged him and said, "Tough fight, Patty you did good." His fight was over and he had nothing to worry about. I thought, *Crap, I wish it was me; I wish my fight was over,* but I did not want to lose. I was hoping Butler wouldn't show up. I thought maybe he would be sick or something, but he was in the locker room. Robbie asked me how I was doing and I said good.

He said, "Listen, I don't want to make you nervous, but there are a lot of people here to see you fight. We brought half of Jersey City with us." Robbie said, "You are going to kick his butt."

They told Robbie to get out of the locker room because only boxers and trainers were allowed. He said, "That is my boy there; he is going to kick some butt." I looked at Butler in the locker room; he was dancing to music on the radio. He was having a good old time. I was thinking about what Anthony told me. I was not going to back up. I knew Butler was tough, but I also knew if I hit him with a right hand, I could knock him out. They called us to fight and as soon as we left the locker room, the crowd started going wild. I thought they were all cheering for Butler but then they started chanting, "Tony, Tony," and I thought, *Great, all these people came to see me get my butt kicked.*

My friends were going nuts, but I did not pay attention to them. I knew this could be the last night of my life. I did not want to get knocked out in front of my friends. We got in the ring, and Butler was huge. I thought, *I am going to have to jump up to punch him.* The bell rang and, as I expected, Butler ran right up to me. He was throwing a lot of punches at me.

I kept my hands up and stayed right in front of him. I was not going to let him back me up. I was blocking the punches but he was punching me so hard he was knocking my own gloves back into my face. I did not know what to do. Then my instincts and all my praying took over. I threw one punch with all I had, and God was helping me because I hit Butler so hard that I knocked him down and he slid on his butt across the ring. All of my friends were going nuts—they were throwing beer up in the air and they were chanting, "Tony, Tony." I kept thinking, *Oh, God, let him stay down on the mat.* The referee counted to five and Butler got up. I knew that he was hurt because I hit him so hard with a solid shot. I could see I hurt him by the look in his eyes. I was not as quick to jump on Butler after he got up because he had me dazed with all the punches he hit me with, and I knew I had to be careful because he was hurt but he was still strong. He was not so quick to run after me, either, not after he felt my right hand.

The bell rang and I went back to my corner. Mr. Weaver was going nuts. He said, "Move your head." The bell rang and I went right at Butler. I could not knock him out because I hit him so hard my right hand felt like it was broken. I had to fight Butler with one hand. After I knocked him down, he was scared. I kept chasing him and throwing left jabs. Butler caught me with a punch and cut me over my right eye. The referee called time and brought me over to the doctor. I kept thinking, *Don't stop the fight because of the cut.* Mr. Weaver and Paulie were yelling at the referee saying, "You had better not stop this fight!" The crowd was yelling, "Don't stop it!" Hollywood was at ringside and he got up and said, "That's my boy," and the referee let me fight. I guess the doctor and the referee did not want to have to deal with Hollywood, Mr. Weaver, Paulie, *and* the crowd. The doctor asked me if I was okay and I said yes. The referee said, "Continue to fight."

I was fighting with one hand and I was just seeing red out of the one eye. The bell for the third round rang and the fight was over. I was the only one that had lasted three rounds with Butler. After the fight, I hugged him and he told me, "You were the only one to last. You're strong." I thanked God that Butler did not knock me out. Mr. Weaver and Paulie were hugging me, saying, "Great fight," and the crowd was on its feet cheering.

We had to wait for the decision. My friends kept on chanting, "Tony, Tony." Then the announcer said, "In the blue corner, from Jersey City, the 1978 Light Heavyweight Champion, Tony." I jumped back to my corner and yelled to Paulie and Mr. Weaver, "We did it, we did it!"

My friends were going nuts—when I got out of the ring they poured beer over my head. I went back to the locker room and my face was so beat up that Chucky was worried about me.

"How do you feel," Tony?" he asked.

Mr. Weaver said, "What do you think? He feels great. He is the New Jersey Golden Glove Champ."

I saw Butler in the locker room. I did not say anything to him because I knew felt bad. I would not have felt bad if they had given the decision to Butler because he fought a tough fight, but I had just heard his manager yell at him. Butler kept saying, "The kid was strong."

Paulie took off my gloves and my right hand was swollen about three times bigger than the normal size. Mr. Weaver looked at the right hand and said, "Now I know why you did not knock him out. Your hand is broken." He said, "You got balls, kid, you fought a tough guy with one hand and one eye."

The boxer that Butler had beaten the week before came over to me on my chair and shook my hand. He said, "I knew you could do it."

"Thanks, you fought really well, too."

Anthony came running up to me and said, "I told you it would work. I told you don't back up."

"Yeah, Anthony, it worked!"

They gave me my golden glove in a little white envelope; I wish the fight could have been a draw because Butler deserved that golden glove just as much as I did.

I drove home with Jake and I was thanking God he let me win the fight. We went to Mulligan's bar. The place was packed and I did not even get to buy a drink because everybody kept buying them for me. When I left, I ordered a case of beer and when I went to give the bartender my money, Mr. Mulligan said, "Don't take his money." I got up the next day and did not know which hurt more: the hangover or the fight. Either way, I felt great.

My mother said, "Well, how did it go?"

I said, "I won."

She jumped up, lifted up her arms, and said, "Way to go, champion!"

Chapter Twenty:

Golden Glove Champ

I partied for two weeks after I won the Golden Gloves. I had worked hard and I needed a break. My mother brought me a gold chain to hang the golden glove around my neck. That golden glove started a lot of street fights. All the tough guys thought if they could beat a Golden Glove champ, they could make a name for themselves. Jake was going to box in my high school gym the Friday night after I won the Golden Gloves. Patty and I drank two quarts of beer and went to see Jake fight. We went back to the dressing room to see Jake and Lefty. Lefty said, "Where the hell have you been? Did you retire?"

"No, Lefty," I said. "I just took a little break. I wanted to let my hand heal before I started to work out. I will be back in the gym on Monday."

They had a light heavyweight they wanted to match up with Jake but Lefty said, "I don't want Jake fighting him, I want you to fight him."

I thought, *Oh, crap, I just finished two quarts of beer and Lefty wants me to fight this guy.* I did not want to tell Lefty I had been drinking so I just said, "Lefty, I have not trained for two weeks and my hand is still swollen." I wanted to tell him to let Jake fight the guy, but I knew Lefty knew boxing and his decision was correct. I did not want to tell Lefty what to do; he had forgotten more about boxing than I knew. Lefty did not let Jake fight and we went home.

Chubs came to my house one Saturday morning with a quart of beer. We started drinking and went to get Chucky. We were sitting up at a park near Chucky's house, drinking beer and talking. Chubs spotted this guy a block away. Chubs said, "That guy over there jumped me with ten of his friends a year ago." Chubs never forgot anything. I had gone with Chubs to the hospital when the kids had jumped him. Chub's mother wanted to take X-rays to make sure nothing was broken. The people at the hospital wanted Chubs to tell who had beaten him up, but he said he had fallen and hit his head. In the hospital, he told me, "I will get them back. I will get them back one day, you wait and see." Back in those days, nobody called the cops; you took care of things on your own.

The guy was in a car, but Chubs took off running. Chucky and I followed him to make sure the guy did not have any friends with him. The guy was stopped at a red light and he had the window of the car down. Chubs ran up to him and started punching him in the face, then he pulled the guy out of the car and kicked him in the head. The whole time Chubs was beating up the guy, Chubs was saying, "Remember me? You were tough when you had ten of your friends with you. You are not so tough now." Chubs beat the crap out of the guy, and then the guy got in his car and left. Chubs came back to us and said, "I knew I would see one of those guys one day. And today was my lucky day."

I told Chubs and Chucky we had to get the hell out of here because the cops would be there soon. We left and went to Mulligan's bar. We were going to a concert that night to see a band that played rock and roll. Jessie Mulligan, Mr. Mulligan's son had bought me a ticket, and he had a bus chartered to take us there. I asked him if Chucky and Chubs could come. He said they could come on the bus, adding, "I do not think they will get in the concert because the tickets are sold out."

We got to the concert and I was drunk. Chucky and Chubs could not get in, but I went without them. After the concert, we all got in the bus and went back to Jersey City. I met Jake near Mulligan's bar and Chucky and Chubs went home.

Jake, Patty, and I went to this bar to have some drinks. It was about 12 AM, and I was talking with Jake and having a good time. Patty was messing around with the barmaid. This guy sitting next to us was trying to pick her up, and he told Patty to leave her alone or he would beat him up. The guy was getting loud with Patty; he would not shut up and he went on and on. Patty kept messing around with the barmaid anyway. Patty was only a little guy and he was just having fun. The guy told Patty again that he was going to beat him up, and I told Jake to whack the guy before he tried to whack Patty. Jake was sitting right next to the guy at the bar. Jake just looked at me and told me to calm down. I said, "Jake, if you don't whack him, I am going to whack him." Jake just shrugged his shoulders. I got up and punched the guy right off his bar stool. A whole barroom brawl started. Patty jumped on the pool table and was whacking guys with a pool stick. Jake and I were whacking whoever got in our way.

We got out of the bar and went to another one, figuring that had been enough fighting for one day. First Chubs got in a fight in the afternoon, then this one. Jake went into the bar and Patty and I were talking to these girls outside when a carload of guys passed us, hanging out of the window screaming at Patty and I. I said, "Patty, ignore them." We kept talking to the girls and the guys came around the block again. They were still yelling and this time they stopped the car. One of them came running at me, and I had no choice: it was fight or get beat up. The guy was running at me full speed so I got in my boxing stance and hit him with a right hand. He hit the ground hard and was hurt.

Patty said, "Man, that is the hardest right hand I ever saw." As soon as he said that, five guys got out of the car, I got thrown on the ground, and they started kicking me. I was looking to see the kicks coming so I could block them when I saw Patty getting thrown into the air. The guys took off in their car when I got up and saw Jake coming out of the bar. He looked at me and said, "I can't leave you alone for five minutes." I went back to Jake's house and we went to sleep.

The next day when I woke up, I noticed my golden glove and the chain my mother had brought me were gone. I said, "Crap, Jake; I cannot find my golden glove."

He said, "Oh, crap, you lost the golden glove." We backtracked all the places we had been the night before, but no glove. I figured I had won it in a fight and lost it in a fight. That golden glove had started many street fights so I figured I was better off without it, but my mother was pissed that I lost the chain. I knew the golden glove was not as important as the memory of the Golden Gloves, but I was mad that I lost the chain my mother bought me.

Jake had been in a lot of trouble in the past. He used to get into fights every day, but he had calmed down a lot and stayed out of trouble. I said, "Jake, when am I going to learn to stay out of trouble?"

"You'll learn," he said. "There comes a point in your life when you don't need the crap anymore. When the time comes, you know you have to change your life."

I knew I was getting sick of the street fights. It seemed like I did not have a choice but to fight.

Jake said, "We messed up that bar pretty good last night. We had better make sure the cops are not looking for us." We went to Mulligan's bar and told Jessie what had happened.

He said, "Just hang low for a few days and my father will take care of it." Mr. Mulligan knew everybody and he made sure the cops did not come after us. He even smoothed things over with the other bar owner. Mr. Mulligan was always a great guy. He took care of the whole bar mess for us and never even mentioned it again. Mr. Mulligan, like a lot of men from Jersey City, was a great guy. The men from Jersey City were real tough guys. Most of them could stare death in the eyes and not be afraid, but hey also had huge hearts and they were full of love.

I had another boxing match coming up so I started training hard. It was July and it was hot. Lefty could tell if you had been drinking alcohol by how much you sweat when you trained. Lefty said to me, "Stay off the oil. Nothing but trouble comes with the oil." I asked him if he drank he said, "No, but I used to tend bar for one of my brothers who owned a bar. Drinking brings a lot of trouble."

Lefty was right—the times I really got in trouble, I was drunk. Drinking had become a monster; everything my friends and I did involved drinking. We did not drink as normal people drink. We thought normal drinking was drinking a twelve-pack of beer or more.

Lefty was the best coach I ever had in my life. He would tell you things and then let you figure things out for yourself. Lefty liked me because I listened to him and when he told me to do something, I did it. If Lefty had a fighter who lost a fight, Lefty would tell him he lost because he did not listen. The fight after the Golden Gloves was in Toms River, New Jersey. Being an amateur boxer is like being a gladiator; you usually don't know who you are going fight until you get to the locker room. This fight was the first time Lefty worked my corner. Paulie drove Lefty and I to Toms River, and Patty came along for the ride. Lefty did not like when I stopped talking before a boxing match. I liked to concentrate but he thought I was nervous. He gave me some water with sugar in it to calm my nerves. I did not want to drink any water, but I had to listen to Lefty. He matched me up to fight this guy from Jersey City. The guy had a big mouth, but I did not listen to him because getting mad is not good for a boxer. Lefty did not like the guy's mouth. He looked at the guy and said, "He will take care of you in the ring." I never thought about the outcome of the fight because you never know what is going to happen. A fight is alive; you cannot control it; you have to be prepared and be ready for anything that happens.

It was nice having Lefty in my corner. Paulie was in the corner, too, but Lefty was a real pro. He worked a corner like a master; he could see mistakes the other boxer was making and tell you what to do to take advantage of them. The ring was in a high school gym about an hour away from Jersey City and it was a week-night so my friends from Jersey City were not there to root me on. That was okay because if I did lose, I did not want them to see it.

During the first round I moved around and hit the guy with jabs. I hit him with a couple of right hands but I really did not rock him. He hit me with a jab, and I found out the guy was pretty strong. The bell rang and I went back to the corner. Lefty was real cool. He said, "You are doing good, but, listen, this guy got a good chin—you got to hit him in the body." I usually did not throw body shots but I knew I was going to do what Lefty told me because if I did not, I would never hear the end of it.

I went out for the second round and hit the guy with a couple of jabs. I hit him with a right hand to the body and I could see it hurt him. I hit him with another right hand to the body and I could hear Lefty saying, "Yeah, yeah." The next punch, I faked a right hand to the body, came up, and hit him on the chin with a solid right hand. The guy went down. Every time I knocked a guy down I always said, "God, let him stay down," but this guy got back up. I could see he was hurt. I hit him with another right hand and knocked him down, and the referee stopped the fight.

Lefty was happy with my performance. He said, "See what happens when you listen to me?" I always listened to my coaches because they knew what they were doing. After the fight, Lefty started telling me, "You could be making a lot of money." I knew as soon as I heard that Lefty wanted me to turn pro. A lot of people told me I needed to have a lot more amateur fights before I turned pro. All I knew is the odds were I would do okay for awhile and then get my butt kicked. I would have nothing to fall back on for employment because I did not have any skills. I saw too many boxers that were really good get their butts kicked. Usually they stopped boxing after that. I always had a business sense about me, so I thought if I could make enough money to open a business, it would be worth getting my butt kicked. Most boxers from Jersey City made from a hundred to a thousand bucks a fight; once in awhile some guys would make five thousand, but they had to fight a really tough boxer and usually they got beat when they fought for the bigger purse. I knew I was at a crossroads.

I went to see my friend Harry box in the Jersey City Armory. Harry was a big black guy who I sparred with in Lefty's Gym. Harry was strong with a muscular body. I really liked him; he would try to kill me while we were sparring but afterwards he was really nice. Harry was the kind of guy you did not want to piss off, but he had a heart of gold. That was the thing I loved about boxing—it did not matter who you were, how much money you had, if you were black, white, or green. All that mattered in boxing was balls and brains, and sometimes balls counted more than brains. Harry had won a couple of professional fights when he was in his first six-round boxing match. I did not think he would have a problem winning because he was so tough. He came out of the dressing room with a red robe on, and he looked big and strong for a light heavyweight. His opponent came out, and the opponent was bigger than Harry. As soon as I saw him, I did not feel good.

Most managers babied their boxers, having them fight guys they knew they would beat. A lot of pros had a record of twenty wins and no losses. This was Harry's fourth professional fight and they were throwing him in the ring with a real tough fighter. Lefty did not like building up the fake records; he got you good money fights and if you won or lost, you made good money. Harry's manager was a real tough guy named Frankie. I always thought he was in the mob because he would take care of someone if he had a problem. He had been a professional fighter in his youth, and Harry was the only fighter that he managed. You could tell Frankie was a fighter by his nose; he had a flat nose, which was a trademark of a boxer that had been through a lot of fights. My mother said, "Those boxers noses look bad; they look like they are not smart people." I did not see it that way. I saw those flat noses as the sign of a true warrior. I really respected the guys with the flat noses. Frankie always carried a gun and he was not afraid to pull out if he needed to get his point across. That night, all I could think of was, *Crap, Frankie put Harry in with this monster for two hundred bucks.*

The bell rang and Harry and his opponent went at it. It was a great fight, too great for two hundred bucks. Harry was hitting the guy hard but the guy was tagging Harry hard also. I was sitting with Patty watching the fight and I told him it was pretty messed up that Frankie put him in there with this guy for two hundred bucks. Patty said, "Frankie ain't wasting no time; he wants to see what Harry is made of." I knew Patty was right but I wanted Harry to have his glory with the easy fighters just like the other guys that had just turned pro.

The bell for the end of the sixth round rung and I did not know if Harry would get the decision. He won the fight but I think it should have been a draw because the both fighters deserved to win. I was just happy Harry won the fight. I went to congratulate him, and he was happy, but I noticed something different in his eyes. I asked him if he was okay and he said he was, so I finished watching all the other scheduled fights. Harry's fight was the best of the night. There is nothing like two warriors going at it. The warriors are putting everything on the line and should be paid well. This night Harry and his opponent were not paid well for the war they had.

I was walking home after the fights, about two blocks from home, when Harry pulled up in a Volkswagen Bug and yelled for me. I went over and he shook my hand. I said, "Good job, Harry, that was a tough fight." I told him, "You had the best fight of the night."

He said, "Yeah, that is my last fight."

I was shocked. I said, "That was your last fight?"

"Yeah. It is different in the pros. They make you use eight-ounce gloves and it is as if you are fighting bare knuckles. Those punches hurt like hell."

Harry was a factory worker and I hated to think of him spending the rest of his life just working in a factory. That was the last time I saw Harry.

I guess he was smarter than the average boxer, though, because he got out before he got his brain messed up. Some boxers from Left's had boxing records of thirty and oh. Some boxers had thirty fights before they would have a war like Harry's. Lefty told me you can only have about three real wars in your boxing career; that is all the normal guy can take. He told me you want to make sure you are paid well for your wars because each one might be your last payday. Most big fights were out of the New Jersey area. You could get paid okay if you fought in Madison Square Garden, but most big paydays were in Vegas. You had to be careful because if you fought out of New Jersey and you did not knock out your opponent, the judges would probably not give you the win on a decision. I saw a welterweight that trained in Left's fight an ex-champion of the world. I thought Nino won the fight but they gave the fight to ex-champion. It happened a lot; fighters would give their hearts and souls in a fight and some judge would rip them off. A judge does not realize how it affects the fighter. Some boxers quit after a bad decision. There were boxers from Left's I saw beat world champions on TV. Most of them got ripped off by bad judges. I don't think anybody should be able to judge a boxing match or commentate on a boxing match unless they were a boxer. I think if a judge rips off a boxer, the audience should be able to vote if the boxer gets to box the judge. If the judge had a chance on getting his butt kicked, you would see a lot better judging. It makes me sick to see a judges rip a boxer off after the boxer gives his heart and soul. And commentators who claim they are boxing experts are not experts. You cannot be a boxing expert unless you know how it feels to get in the ring and put everything on the line. You can always tell who is the boxing expert when you watch a fight on TV. Boxing experts are slow to criticize a boxer because they know how hard it is to get in the ring and fight. The real boxing expert gets pissed off when a fight is judged badly because they know how much work it takes to win a fight. A so-called boxing expert does not know this. They want to see boxers punch the crap out of each other because they have never felt that hard punch themselves.

After Harry's fight, I was really thinking, *What the hell am I going to do? I do not have any skill to work with. All I know is how to do is fight.* I knew I did not want to work in a factory job or another crap job for the rest of my life. I did not know what the hell I was going to do. I got a call from a friend one day; this girl I used to date was asking for me. He said her uncle wanted to get a hold of me to see if I wanted a job, but I'd have to carry a gun. Her uncle owned a club in New York and my friend told me he would pay me twenty-five dollars an hour. I thought, *Crap, twenty-five bucks an hour is great.* I think the guy was connected to the mob and I did not know what the hell I was going to have to do for the money. I did not really like guns because I did enough damage with my hands. I asked my mother about taking the job. She said, "Oh, crap don't take that job. They will have you killing people before you know it." I had a quick temper and knew if I had a gun and somebody pissed me off, I would shoot him. I did not want to kill anybody; I always thought about the electric chair stories my mother had told me as a kid. My mother told me, "Listen, I told you to stop messing around with that girl because if you knock her up, they are going to cut your pecker off." I hated to turn the twenty-five bucks an hour down, but I knew it was going to lead to a life I did not want. I loved my mother too much to live a life of crime.

I was just hanging out in my house and the doorbell rang. It was Patty. I said, "What's up, Patty?"

He said, "I just got back from New York."

"Come on in the house, Patty." My mother was in the kitchen. I loved talking to Patty because he always had something to make me laugh. "What were you doing in New York?"

"I was trying to get laid." Patty was obsessed with trying to getting laid.

I said, "So, did you get laid?"

He said, "No. I saw this guy and he asked me if I wanted to get laid and I said yes. He said, 'Okay, give me twenty bucks and go up to the second floor.'" Patty said, "I gave the guy twenty bucks and went up to the second floor and it was a vacant building. That guy beat me for my money." I was laughing my butt off. Then Patty told me, "I went to this club. You pay twenty bucks to get in and these girls give you a rubdown like a massage. I got this nice girl. Then she asked me if I wanted to get laid. I said yes so she told me it was going to cost me seventy-five bucks. I said, 'Holy crap, I am not going to pay seventy-five bucks to get laid!' Patty asked me, "When the hell am I going to get laid?"

"Never, the way you are going. Next time, see the girl before you give the money."

"Yeah, that makes sense," he said.

I went to the bar to have a couple of drinks and see my old friend Tex. He said, "Let's go to this dance club to try and pick up some girls." We went to the dance club and did not do too good with the girls; we just got drunk. After awhile he said, "Let's go home," and we started to drive home. I was almost sleeping in the car when Tex said I am going to make a stop to get some tires." He stopped in this junkyard to steal some tires and I was so drunk I just stayed in the car. I fell asleep and all of a sudden I hard a click. I woke up and this cop had his gun touching the top of my head. He said, "What are you doing?"

"Man, I'm just sleeping," I said.

"This your car?"

I said no, and then they heard Tex in the junkyard. They told me to get him out of there or they were going to start shooting. I yelled, "Come on, Tex, get out or they are going to shoot at you."

The cops started yelling, and Tex finally came out. There were five big, mean dogs in the junkyard and the cops were afraid to go in there. When Tex came out, the cops asked him if he was afraid of the dogs and he said no. "The dogs barked at me, I looked at them and said, 'Get the hell out of here,' and they left."

Tex was pissed he got busted. He said, "Sorry, Tony."

I said, "It happens sometimes, Tex."

The cops took us to the jailhouse and booked us. Tex was giving them a hard time. He did not want to give them his address so he told them he lived at 3535 Mocking Bird Lane. I told the cops my name and address and they were nice to me. They told me to go in this room and the last thing I saw was a cop with a nightstick and a telephone book going after Tex. I heard a loud noise like the cop put the phone book over Tex's head and was pounding him with the nightstick. There was nothing I could do to help him. They put him in a room with me and I said, "Listen, Tex, I have had enough fun for one night. Tell the cops your address." The way I looked at it was that once the cops caught us, the game was over. The worst thing we could do was piss them off. Tex gave them his address.

The cops brought us to the cells. There was one guy in the middle one of the three cells. When we walked in the guy said, "Man, am I glad to see you guys. I have been here since Friday. You guys are lucky; you get to see the judge tomorrow. I have been by myself since Friday, and I just turned eighteen years old Friday." He said, "They caught me shoplifting and they would not let me go. My mother did not bail me out; she told me to wait to see the judge."

As soon as he said that I said, "Crap, my mother is going to be mad."

Tex did not give a crap because he had been arrested many times before. All I could think about was hurting my mother. This kid kept talking and talking. He said he was getting strong because he had been doing push-ups all weekend long. This cop came in and told Tex, "I am not giving you a blanket because you are a jerk." He asked me if I wanted one, and since it was a cold night, I said yes. He threw me a blanket that had shit all over it.

I said, "Oh, crap, this jail business is not for me." I started thinking that I had to make a change in my life. See, it is like my mother always says—you always get what is coming to you. You see, I really did not do anything wrong that night. I should not have been locked up. However, I had done a lot of bad stuff in the past that I did not pay for, and now I was paying the price.

This kid kept talking, and I told him to shut the hell up and go to sleep. The next day the cops woke us up and said it was time to see the judge. A detective drove us to the courthouse and when we got there they put us in with all of these guys who had been busted for robbing cars or fighting.

This lawyer came in and asked Tex and me what happened. We told him the story about Tex being in the junkyard and me sleeping. The lawyer asked me if I went in to the property and I said no. The lawyer told me they did not have anything on me. He said, "Do not worry."

Tex and I went before the judge and the lawyer told Tex to plead guilty and he would get off with a fine. The prosecutor was cool; he told the judge I did not do anything and the judge let me go. The judge told me to stay out of trouble. They gave Tex a two-hundred dollar fine. I got home and my mother was mad even though I told her I was sorry. I knew I had to stay out of trouble because I did not want to disappoint her.

Two weeks later, I was drinking with my friend Red. Red was a good kid who liked fishing and hunting. He stayed out of trouble so I figured I wouldn't get into trouble, either. I was staying away from my friends that like to get in trouble. It was about midnight and Red and I were having a good time walking down the street when we saw a kid that we knew. The kid was a quarterback for a local high school, and he was drunk. We passed him and just said, "What's up?"

He said to Red, "I know you. You ratted on my friend after he stole some gas."

Red said, "Yeah, he stole the gas from me and if I did not rat on him, I would have had to pay for it."

The kid looked at Red and said, "I am going to kick your butt."

I said, "You are not going to kick nobody's butt."

"I am going to kick both of your butts."

Red did not know how to fight. The kid came at me and threw a punch so I started fighting with him. I hit him with a couple of jabs then I hit him with a right hand and knocked him off his feet. When he hit the ground, the back of his head smashed against the sidewalk and he did not get up. Red and I were walking away, but a man down the block had been watching the fight and when we got to the corner, he said, "You had better go check on the guy."

I said, "He started the fight."

He said, "Yeah, but at least go see if you killed him."

The kid was out cold. I shook him and he started crying for his mother. I heard some people do that before they die so I thought, *Oh, crap.* I told him to get up and he snapped out of it. He jumped up and ran to a parked car, grabbed an antenna, and started chasing Red and me. I told Red to run because I knew if I hit the kid again, I would kill him. We ran to Red's basement and slept there. We heard the cop cars all over the place and I knew they were looking for us. All I could think about was, *Look at this crap—this kid wanted to fight, he was going to beat the crap out of Red and me, and now he called the cops.* Crap like that usually did not happen in Jersey City. Usually if you were man enough to put up your hands up, you took your butt-kicking and did not call the cops.

I went home the next morning and my mother was mad. She said, "Get your clothes and get out of here. The cops were here looking for you."

"Don't you even want to know what happened?" I asked. "This guy threw a punch at me and I kicked his butt."

She just said, "Call the cops; they are looking for you."

I said, "No, it is Saturday and I won't see the judge until Monday. I will just stay low and go to the police station on Monday."

She said okay, so I went to the police station on Monday and told the cops what had happened. The cops said the kid had to go to the hospital because he had a concussion. They took me to see the judge and I got the same judge as I had when I got busted with Tex. I had the same prosecutor, too. They charged me with attempted murder and I said, "What? I hit the kid with one punch after he threw a punch at me."

The cops said, "The kid said you and two other kids beat him up."

I said, "That is a lie." I told the cops the true story and said, "I have a right to defend myself, don't I?"

The judge asked me if I had ever been arrested before. I looked at the prosecutor and he was shaking his head yes. I said, "Yes, sir, I have been arrested before."

The judge said, "Yes, I remember you, I told you to stay out of trouble. I am giving you your last chance. I am going to give you a lesser charge but if I see you in here again, I am going to send you away to jail." He gave me a court date and released me. I knew this was it. My luck was changing. I had to do something. I went to Mulligan's and told my friend Robbie what had happened.

Robbie said, "Yeah, that kid came in here and I told him you were my friend. I told him if he called the cops, we'd kill him. Want me to take care of him?"

I said, "No, Robbie, I don't want to have the kid killed. Don't you think they would know I had something to do with this? I do not need any more problems." I told Robbie to leave it be and I would take care off it. Robbie scared the kid so bad he did not even show up to court. My mother went to court with me and the kid's father was in the courtroom. The lawyer worked a deal out with the judge. I had to pay the doctor bills and the kid would drop the charges. The kid's father started telling me some crap about fighting. My mother looked at him and said, "Tell your son not to put up his hands if he can not take a butt-kicking."

I went home and thought good and long. One thing boxing had taught me is that if you are getting your butt kicked, you have to turn things around. I was getting my butt kicked in a different way; I had been arrested twice within a month. I knew I could not stay out of trouble in Jersey City. There was too much trouble around, and I could not stay in my house for the rest of my life. That was the only way I knew how to stay out of trouble. I knew if I got in trouble again, the judge would have to lock me up. I did not blame the judge; he was actually nice to me. He had given me two chances and it was up to me to make some changes or I was headed for jail. I knew it would not be long until my first test of staying out of trouble came.

I stayed in my house for about a week. It got boring. I met some friends that did not get in trouble as much as my friends from Thirty-three Schoolyard. We went to a bar in the neighborhood and we were having a good time until this guy showed up. He had just gotten out of jail and he wanted to fight. He was pushing people around the bar and he was being rude to the girls sitting there. He kept staring at me. Usually that was all it would have taken—I would have hit the guy before he knew what was coming. He looked like a real tough guy, but I would have beaten his butt in no time at all. I would have loved to beat the crap out of the guy but I just kept thinking about the judge. I thought of Jake telling me that I would know when it was time to start staying out of trouble. As much as I would have loved to punch this tough guy, I decided I had to stay out of trouble. I sat at the bar and thought about what I was going to do. I told my friends I had to go home and I said good night. I walked up to the tough guy and looked him straight in the eyes. He said, "You got a problem?"

I said, "No, I don't have a problem, tough guy." I walked out of the bar and did not look back. That was the first time in a long time I passed up a fight. I left the bar and went home. I was mad; there was no way I could stay in Jersey City and stay out of trouble. I hated passing up a chance to kick somebody's butt when he deserved it, but boxing had taught me to stick with my strategy and I knew it was hard but I had to stay out of trouble.

Friday night I decided to go out with my sister and some of her friends. My sister had a good time and hung out with a mellow crowd so I felt like I could stay out of trouble with her. We went to a nightclub and had a good time. There was this older guy at the bar and he was telling me jokes. It was the first time I had been in a club in awhile and I did not get into trouble. My sister and her friends asked me if I wanted to go to China Town in New York to eat. I asked them just to drop me off near my house so I could go to White Castle.

They dropped me off at my mother's house and I walked around the corner to White Castle. I ate some hamburgers and started to walk home. I saw these three guys walking towards me and I knew my nice night was coming to an end. The guys asked me for a quarter. I had about two hundred bucks in my pocket and I knew if I gave them a quarter they would rob me. I told them I did not have a quarter. I was ready to fight the three of them before I was going to give them my two hundred bucks. One of the guys pulled a gun on me. I got a head rush and started laughing. I said, "I don't have no quarter." I said, "You want to shoot me, shoot me, but you are not getting a quarter." He put the gun back in his pants and I walked away but I was really pissed. I went home and got a baseball bat. I knew the three guys were going to White Castle and I was going to wait until they started eating and run in White Castle and bust the three of their heads open for pulling that gun on me. Then I started thinking, *If I do that, I will have to see the judge and he is going to send me away.* You see, those three guys deserved to get their heads busted. However, if I had busted their heads, I would have gone to jail. I put the bat back and went to lie down. It took me a long time to go to sleep because I was so pissed off. You see, if I had not gotten into trouble and I wasn't worried about that judge, there was no question I would have busted their heads open. It did not matter that they had a gun. My bat and I could have beaten the three of those guys and their gun.

I got up the next day and told my mother what had happened. She said, "Yes, if you had busted their heads open, you would be the one that went to jail."

One time my sister's friend had to go to court because he beat this guy up. The judge fined my him, and his father stood up in court and said, "Your honor, what happened to the day when you could kick somebody's butt when they deserved it?" He had summed it all up; times were changing in Jersey City. I had been in hundreds of street fights and the cops were never called. Now I could not even defend myself without going to jail. I knew I had to do something.

Chapter Twenty-one:

Getting Out

I was at home watching a movie on TV about this hippy that had joined the Marines. I said, "That is it, I have to get out of here. I can join the Marines." I called my father. I did not talk a lot with my father but when I needed some advice I would listen to him because he was usually right. He had been in the Korean War so he knew about the military. I did not know anything about it. All I knew were the movies and recruiting commercials and I knew neither one of them was telling the truth. I told my father I was getting in a lot of trouble and I had to get out of the city. I said, "I am thinking about joining the Marines."

I thought he would be happy but he said, "If you join the Marines, I am going to kick the crap out of you."

My father was in the war and he saw a lot of people get killed. I think he killed a lot of people. He had post-traumatic stress; if he heard a firecracker on the Fourth of July, he hit the ground quickly. It was sad that somebody like my father could not even enjoy the Fourth of July after he had put it all on the line for his country. The war had ruined my father's life. He said, "I do not want you to join any branch in the military because they treat you like crap. I did enough for the country for my whole family. I do not want you to go through the same crap as I had to go through." He said, "If you need to join any of the branches of the service, join the Air Force. They have it the best." I listened to him and went to see the Air Force recruiter. They had my test scores from high school on file and my scores were too low to get into the Air Force, but I told the recruiter let me take the test over. The first time, I had just guessed and picked any answer. The recruiter gave me some material to study and I took it home. I studied and prayed. I said, "God, you know I have to get out of here."

Well, God answered my prayers and I got a high enough score to get into the Air Force. The recruiter told me that I was going to basic training in two weeks.

I went home and told my mother I was leaving in two weeks. She said, "You are leaving in two weeks—that is too fast."

I said, "I have to go, Mom." I hated leaving my mother, family, and friends, but I had always wanted to have a wife and kids. I knew if I did not get out of the city, I would spend the rest of my life in and out of jail or dead. I called Lefty and he was mad. He said, "You could make a lot of money boxing."

I said, "Lefty, I have no skills. I have to learn something because I do not want to work in a factory for the rest of my life."

He pleaded with me not to go, but I told him I had already signed the contract. I said, "Please don't be mad at me, Lefty, it is something I have to do."

I told all of my friends I was leaving.

My friends from Thirty-three Schoolyard planned a big party for me the night before I left for basic training. I had to be in Newark at 8 AM, and I knew it would be a wild party. I went to Mulligan's where all of my friends were. We had a great time. They had all of these little shot glasses lined up on the bar and one big glass for me in the middle. We all got drunk and talked about good old times. They made a book for me with everybody's address so I could write to them from basic training. I went to my friend's house to sleep and woke up at 6 AM. I ran home and my mother had my suitcase packed; I had to run.

My mother kissed me goodbye and said, "Promise me two things."

I said, "What, Mom?"

She said, "Do not get married and do not get a tattoo."

I said, "Okay, Mom," and I ran to the train station. Leaving my mother was the hardest thing I ever did in my life. I had a pain in my stomach the whole train ride to Newark, but I got there on time with a bad hangover. I was happy I had partied with all my friends because I knew it would be my last party for a while.

They enlisted twenty of us and gave us a package and plane tickets for Texas. I had never been out of the New Jersey-New York-Pennsylvania area before and it was the first time I was on a plane. I was the only person from Jersey City. It was a nice trip but I knew basic training was going to be like jail.

This drill sergeant was yelling at us as soon as we got out of the bus. They lined us up in a military formation. There were guys from all over the country. I was laughing listening to the accents of people from different parts of the country. I had never been exposed to different accents before. This little drill sergeant got in my face and started yelling at me and calling me names. My first reaction was to step out of the line and beat the crap out of him, but I thought quick and said to myself, *You came here to get out of trouble and if you beat this drill sergeant up, you will wind up back in Jersey City.* I bit my tongue and stayed in the line and let the drill sergeant yell at me. Basic training sucked, but I knew from my boxing training that you had to take the good with the bad to get what you wanted. I liked to shoot the guns. I had only shot a gun once before, with my father when he took us to the mountains. He said, "You got to know how to shoot because if they send you to war, it is them or you."

The first time I shot the M16 the instructor put the target out twenty-five yards out and told me to fire ten shots. I fired my ten shots and the instructor pulled the target in. He said, "I have to adjust your sights."

I asked why and he said, "All of your shots are in the head."

I said, "Yes, I know, that is were I am aiming."

"Where are you from?" he asked.

"Jersey City."

"That figures. You have to aim for the stomach."

The military was good to me. They taught me how to use my mind and not my fists to solve problems. The military had strict rules but it provided a safe place to live and to raise a family. I learned a trade that has earned me a living, and I fulfilled my dream of having a big family. After twenty years in the service, I have a wife and six kids. I had a lot of exciting experiences and visited different parts of the world, but that is another story. I did not become a famous boxer, but I stayed out of jail. I never met friends like the ones I had in Jersey City, but a lot of those guys died too early. I keep in touch with the rest; time and distance did not kill the love we have for one another.

Jersey City was a tough place to grow up. We made it harder than it had to be, but we were young. I always thank God for the chances he gave me to turn my life around. We had an old saying in Jersey City: "Nobody is perfect; everybody messes up now and then." The trick of life is not to make the same mistake twice. If you are in a situation where you here a voice telling you to leave, get the hell out of that situation. Change your life. It is up to you what you do with it.

978-0-595-42295-1
0-595-42295-0

www.ingramcontent.com/pod-product-compliance
Lightning Source LLC
Chambersburg PA
CBHW051421280526
45785CB00003B/1113